A WIDER WORLD

A WIDER WORLD

Collections of Foreign Ethnography in Scotland

Edited by Elizabeth I Kwasnik

NATIONAL MUSEUMS OF SCOTLAND
in association with
SCOTTISH MUSEUMS COUNCIL

Front cover: Kwakiutl mask, British Columbia, by Richard Hunt, 1971
Royal Scots Regimental Museum

Frontispiece: Australian Aborigine bark painting of a crocodile, Arnhemland, by George Djayhgurrnga, 1979
National Museums of Scotland

Published by the National Museums of Scotland, Chambers Street, Edinburgh EH1 1JF in association with the Scottish Museums Council

British Library Cataloguing-in-Publication Data
A catalogue record of this book is available from the British Library

ISBN 0 948636 56 4

Designed by the Publications Office, National Museums of Scotland

Printed by Alna Press Ltd, Broxburn

Contents

Part IV: Summary and Recommendations

Appendices

List of Figures:

List of Illustrations:

A Message from Sir David Attenborough

The material that has been surveyed in the preparation
of this volume and recorded in the National Database
comes from the many parts of the world to which
Scottish men and women travelled, often at times when
their journeys were not nearly as easy as they would be
nowadays. The objects they brought back record ways of
life that have almost entirely disappeared under the
impact of western technology and are now irreplaceable.
They are therefore not only of great popular interest but
also have great historical and scientific value.

The museum authorities charged with their care bear a
double responsibility for this heritage. Firstly there is the
international dimension – these objects are clearly part of
the history of the peoples whose ancestors made them
and of which we ought all to be more aware. Secondly,
there is the local dimension – for many of the descen-
dants of those who made, owned and cherished these
objects are now fellow members of our own society.

This volume suggests ways of caring for this important
body of material and also of how it can best be used to
benefit the whole community.

Preface

In many ways, Scotland's history is written through the nation's contacts with the world beyond; contacts which have been made through trade and industry, education and training, medicine and religion, and colonial service and wars over many centuries. One record of these contacts is provided by the collections of foreign ethnographic material housed in museums throughout the length and breadth of the country. They reflect the interest shown in the world at large by Scottish men and women over the centuries and as such are a vital part of Scotland's heritage as well as the world's heritage.

This book records how that heritage has been surveyed and documented nationally for the first time, how museums look after it and make it accessible to public audiences, and what steps we must now take to safeguard it for future generations.

The Foreign Ethnographic Collections Research Programme forms one of a series of national collections research programmes which the Scottish Museums Council has undertaken in recent years in collaboration with the National Museums of Scotland. It was coordinated by a Management Committee whose work relied on the cooperation of many museums in Scotland and ethnography specialists in the United Kingdom, and to all of these we owe a very great debt of thanks for their support.

The results of the Programme are in two parts. The first is an extensive database derived from the fieldwork and research carried out by the Programme Coordinator in conjunction with many specialists in different fields of foreign ethnography. This is part of the National Museums of Scotland national database development. The second is a publication which provides a point of entry into that database and explains how museums can provide enhanced standards of care and presentation for their foreign ethnographic collections. Museums contributing to the Programme have also received copies of database entries for collections management purposes. The Programme has thus not only charted foreign ethnographic collections in museums throughout Scotland, but has also helped museums develop new strategies for the ways in which those collections are to be managed for the future.

The Programme could not have been achieved without the very generous support of the Economic and Social Research Council which provided funding for the appointment of the Programme Coordinator and the Programme Assistant over the two-year period. This is the first time that a programme of this kind has been supported by the ESRC and we are most grateful for their assistance.

Our thanks are also due to Professor Frank Willett, who has himself made such a distinctive contribution to the study of foreign ethnography and who has chaired the Programme's Management Committee.

Timothy Ambrose
Director
Scottish Museums Council

Mark Jones
Director
National Museums of Scotland

Foreword

On behalf of the committee which managed this project, I should like to thank the Economic and Social Research Council for the funding that made the programme possible. Without the grant which enabled us to employ a full-time ethnographer with a half-time Programme Assistant, the project could certainly not have been undertaken, since specialists in foreign ethnography, in Scotland as elsewhere, are very rare.

Indeed, the Programme has served to draw to our attention how few of these collections are cared for by professional ethnographers. The most experienced ethnographers in Scotland are fully employed as senior museum managers with all too little time for direct contact with the collections, as I can vouch for from my own experience when directing the Hunterian Museum and Art Gallery of the University of Glasgow.

A number of ethnographic collections in Scotland are cared for by archaeologists, who at least have some acquaintance with artefacts from other ways of life, but there is an urgent need, despite the restraints of the present economic climate, for the provision of more dedicated posts for curators of foreign ethnography to take care of the larger collections.

I hope that this book will encourage those who have such an irreplaceable archive in their care to seek appropriate advice and develop the often unrealised opportunities offered by collections of foreign ethnography.

Professor Frank Willett
Chairman
Foreign Ethnographic Collections Research Programme

The Foreign Ethnographic Collections Research Programme

Management Committee:

Professor Frank Willett (Chair), formerly Director of the Hunterian Museum and Art Gallery of the University of Glasgow

Dale Idiens (Principal Investigator), Depute Director (Collections) and Keeper of the Department of History and Applied Art, National Museums of Scotland

Timothy Ambrose, Director, Scottish Museums Council

John Burnett, Head of the Library and Documentation Service, National Museums of Scotland

Ian O Morrison, Scottish Museums Documentation Officer, National Museums of Scotland

Barbara Woroncow, Director, Yorkshire and Humberside Museums Council

Programme Staff:

Elizabeth I Kwasnik, Programme Coordinator

Sam Roger, Programme Assistant

Acknowledgements

The Management Committee of the Foreign Ethnographic Collections Research Programme acknowledges the support and cooperation of the many museums, institutions and individuals who have partici- pated in the Programme. The Programme was possible only with the support of the Economic and Social Research Council's Award Number R00232461. The advice and guidance offered in the application process and the generous award are gratefully acknowledged.

The Committee is also indebted to Dale Idiens, Keith Nicklin, Jill Salmons, Jennifer Scarce, Jane Wilkinson and Frank Willett who gave of their time and ethno- graphic knowledge in the capacity of specialist consul- tants. A number of the staff in the National Museums of Scotland have assisted with object identification.

The National Museums of Scotland and the Scottish Museums Council have between them made their libraries, and documentation, information and adminis- trative resources available. A programme of this scale, requiring such a range of expertise, would not have been possible without such a partnership. Acknowledgement is due to Ian O Morrison, Scottish Museums Documentation Officer, National Museums of Scotland, for acting as computing adviser, developing the software, and extracting and compiling the collections data pre- sented in this report. The support given by the University of Glasgow to the Programme, especially in the early stages, was crucial.

The professionalism of Scotland's curators, their cooper- ation and commitment to the collections in their care enabled the Programme to succeed. The Committee is grateful to Sir David Attenborough for his kind message and to Lady Attenborough for taking his photograph specially for this book.

PART I: COLLECTIONS OF FOREIGN ETHNOGRAPHY IN SCOTLAND

A Wider World

Dale Idiens

The numerous and diverse collections of ethnographic material from Africa, Asia, Oceania and the Americas to be found today throughout Scotland are a tangible reflection of Scottish interests and activities all over the world. The national database currently has records of almost 90,000 artefacts held in 53 separate collections in Scotland. The largest collection of 39,022 items is in the National Museums of Scotland. Some of the smallest have no more than one item. Overall, the greatest proportion of material originates from Asia, followed by Africa, Oceania and the Americas. The majority of these objects were collected by Scots between the early nineteenth century and early twentieth century.

Although a small country, Scotland has throughout its history produced a disproportionately large number of individuals who have sought opportunities far from home, whether as explorers, entrepreneurs, doctors, missionaries, soldiers, or colonial officials. Many returned to Scotland after travelling and working abroad, but many more settled permanently elsewhere. The artefacts they acquired, whether picked up as random souvenirs or gathered to meet systematic collecting objectives, today represent important evidence of the past of other societies. They are also a significant part of the heritage of Scotland, and form the major element in most existing collections of foreign ethnography.

The dominant motive for the activities of Scots overseas has always been trade. Missionary zeal, scientific enquiry and colonial interests, while important, were subsidiary. Among the earliest of Scottish commercial activities conducted outside Europe was the whaling industry. Whaling fleets were already established in Scotland's east coast ports by the middle of the eighteenth century. These developed and flourished, continuing in places such as Dundee well into the twentieth century. Scottish whaling vessels regularly operated off the coasts of Greenland and eastern Canada during summer when the pack ice was temporarily reduced. As a result the crews made contact with the indigenous peoples of these areas, the Inuit, and traded with them. Scots had been aware of the Inuit since the sixteenth century, and there is evidence that occasional Inuit kayakers, perhaps blown off-course, had been sighted near Orkney in the seventeenth century. In 1700 there is a recorded instance of an Inuit in a kayak who was encountered off the northeast coast near the Don River and brought to Aberdeen where he died soon afterwards. His kayak, the earliest known in

Scotland, is in the Marischal Museum, Aberdeen. Few Inuit objects in Scotland can be proved to be as early as this owing to lack of contemporary documentation. The Hunterian Museum and Art Gallery, University of Glasgow, has some eighteenth-century Inuit pieces, and several museums, including those in Edinburgh, Perth, Dundee, Peterhead, and Aberdeen, have substantial nineteenth-century Inuit collections. The majority of the material in Scottish collections is from the Eastern Inuit, who occupy the area from Greenland to Hudson Bay.

As the margins of European contact expanded in the seventeenth and eighteenth centuries trading companies such as the East India Company and the Hudson's Bay Company were founded. By the nineteenth century many of these had developed into powerful and influential organisations, sometimes backed by military authority. Their expansion spearheaded the exploration and mapping of parts of the world hitherto unknown to Europeans. Scots were numerous in such trading organisations and occupied positions at all levels. In Canada the staff of the Hudson's Bay Company in the eighteenth and nineteenth centuries were predominantly Scots, drawn especially from Orcadians who joined Bay ships in Stromness as they made their last landfall before crossing the Atlantic. Likewise, many Scots found employment in the East India Company and in the British Army in India. A tradition of Scottish predominance in the Indian Civil Service was established by Henry Dundas, Viscount Melville (1762-1811), while he was President of the Board of Control for India, and Scotland contributed at least two Governor-Generals of India during the nineteenth century.

The impulse for exploration, while ostensibly scientific, was in reality primarily commercial. Scottish explorers were at the forefront of European penetration into many parts of the world in the eighteenth and nineteenth centuries. The objects they collected, from peoples who had little, if any, previous contact with white people, are of particular importance as historic records. The great Pacific navigator, Captain James Cook, although born in Yorkshire, was of Scots descent, and employed many Scots on his voyages of exploration. In North America, Alexander Mackenzie opened up the vast Northwest Territories and Dr John Rae completed the charting of the Arctic Coast. In Africa, James Bruce of Kinnaird discovered the source of the Blue Nile in 1770, and

Mungo Park, the Selkirk surgeon, reached the Niger River in 1795. They were followed in the nineteenth century by Captain Hugh Clapperton who, in 1823, discovered Lake Chad, and W B Baikie, sent by the British Government to explore the Benue and Niger rivers in 1852. James Grant from Nairn accompanied John Speke, the discoverer of the source of the Nile, in East Africa. These explorers, and many others, opened the way for trade. For example, by the mid-nineteenth century Scottish merchants were involved in commerce in the Niger Delta, dealing in palm oil, used for the production of soap and margarine, which replaced the trade in slaves after this was abolished by Britain in 1807.

The most famous Scottish figure in Africa is of course the explorer and missionary David Livingstone who dedicated his life to the elimination of the slave trade in the African hinterland by introducing 'commerce and Christianity'. He inspired generations of Scots missionaries who took the Christian faith to all parts of the world. Missionary associations began to develop in Scotland at the end of the eighteenth century. During the nineteenth century a former mill girl from Dundee, Mary Slessor, established a mission school at Arochuku near Calabar, and after Livingstone's death in 1873 Scottish missionary stations were founded in Nyasaland (now Malawi). Business and commercial concerns developed alongside missionary activity. For example, in Nyasaland, Scottish businessmen established tobacco and tea plantations. Scottish missionaries and businessmen were also active in the Pacific during the nineteenth century. One of the first missionaries in Fiji was an Aberdonian, David Cargill, in 1832. The first British Governor of Fiji, Sir Arthur Gordon, arrived in 1874. With him was Dr (later Sir) William MacGregor, a former farm labourer from Aberdeenshire and a remarkable individual who was to govern four colonies, British New Guinea, Lagos, Newfoundland and Queensland. George Darsie, of Anstruther in Fife, ran a business in Tahiti and in 1878 married a Tahitian princess. The couple eventually retired to Scotland and are buried in Anstruther. Missionary penetration of Asia and the Far East, although beginning somewhat later than in Africa and the Pacific, continued well into the present century. Once again the activities of Scots missionaries, such as Mrs Robert Cunningham and Annie Ross Taylor in Tibet, and medical men like Dr J G Cormack in China and Dr N Gordon Munro among the Ainu in Japan, led to collections which have been deposited in museums in Scotland.

Further collections were formed as a result of military action by British forces. In Africa, such actions included the Ashanti Wars, the punitive expedition to the City of Benin, and the Zulu Wars. Elsewhere, the Younghusband Expedition to Tibet in 1903, the activities of General Sir A J F Reid in the Hindu Kush and on the North West Frontier, and of General Sir L R MacDonald in Tibet and Uganda also led to artefacts

from these areas reaching Scotland. Objects seized as a result of military action were sometimes incorporated into regimental museums. Sometimes intervention was more benign, like that of Major General Sir Robert Murdoch Smith, who directed and developed telegraph communications in Persia from 1865-88.

Links between Scotland and Japan developed rapidly following the first British treaty with Japan, negotiated by Lord Elgin in 1858. The Japanese needed to modernise, especially in the field of industry, and many Scottish engineers seized the opportunity to work in Japan as consultants and teachers. One of the first Scottish companies to become established in Japan was Jardine Mathieson in 1859. Thomas Glover, an Aberdonian who arrived in Japan as an employee of Jardine Mathieson, went on to make a significant contribution, through shipbuilding and coal mining, to Japanese industrial development. In 1872 a major Japanese trade mission visited Scotland, and as a result a young Glasgow engineer, Henry Dyer, was appointed head of the Imperial College of Engineering in Tokyo. Contacts like these led to collections by individuals and institutions, and to exchanges, bringing about a considerable exposure of Japanese art and design in Scotland. This had a discernible influence upon the work of several Scottish artists of the period.

Following the success of the Great Exhibition of 1851 in the Crystal Palace, London, which brought together arts and manufactures from all over the world, there was a dramatic growth in the popularity of exhibitions to stimulate trade between Victorian Britain and world markets. These occasions provided an opportunity for items to be added to museum collections. Glasgow Museums made a major purchase from the Colonial and Indian Exhibition of 1886 in London. In 1888 Glasgow hosted its own international exhibition, with large trade courts exhibiting wares from India, Burma and Ceylon from which purchases were made for Glasgow Museums. Japanese material purchased at the Philadelphia International Exhibition in 1876 had already been added to the Industrial Museum of Scotland, now the National Museums of Scotland.

Early Scottish interest in artefacts of foreign origin had focused chiefly upon the curiosity value of the pieces. The objects were collected as exotic souvenirs, admired for unusual forms or for the use of strange and rare materials. There was little interest in accurate documentation, information about function and use, or appreciation of aesthetic qualities. Collectors concentrated upon elaborate or bizarre items and everyday objects were overlooked. During the seventeenth century, 'cabinets of curiosities' were established by individual antiquarians in Scotland, as elsewhere in Europe. Among notable examples were those of Sir Andrew Balfour and Sir James Sibbald, whose private collections eventually formed the basis of the University of Edinburgh's Museum of

Natural History. The Hunterian Museum and Art Gallery, University of Glasgow, developed from the large and wide-ranging collection amassed on a scholarly basis by William Hunter, a successful doctor and teacher, in the mid-eighteenth century.

By the late eighteenth century, associations of antiquarian collectors were beginning to be formed. The earliest in Scotland was the Society of Antiquaries of Scotland, founded in Edinburgh in 1780. The Perth Literary and Antiquarian Society started in 1784 and many others followed. This trend coincided with a new expansion of Europeans into Asia, the Pacific, Africa and the Americas and provided homes for some of the earliest foreign ethnography that may still be identified today. The collections of Scottish and foreign antiquities created by such societies frequently provided the basis for museums. Material from the voyages of Captain James Cook found its way into the collections of the Society of Antiquaries of Scotland and is now in the National Museums of Scotland. Other important Pacific artefacts were given to the Perth Society by David Ramsay.

From the eighteenth century onwards a number of universities in Scotland were also active in collecting foreign ethnographic material. Professors of natural history established collections of zoological material for teaching purposes, often incorporating items of foreign ethnography. Edinburgh University's Natural History Museum, for example, was based upon two seventeenth-century cabinets. This collection contained important early material but its care and condition were often haphazard. The Professor of Natural History had to pay for the maintenance, heating and staff of the museum out of his own pocket. Costs were recovered by entrance charges to the public and, sometimes, by selling off parts of the collection. In 1780 Professor John Walker started to reorganise the collections. He was followed by Professor Robert Jameson (1804-1854), a remarkable individual who developed the museum to rank with the best in Europe. Jameson enlarged the museum by actively soliciting collections from former students abroad and engaging official government support to enable collections to be sent to Edinburgh. In this way he obtained Inuit material acquired by Royal Navy expeditions in search of the Northwest Passage, including those by Captain John Ross, Edward Parry and Frederick Beechey. Jameson issued collecting instructions and advice on packing and transport to potential collectors but despite these efforts much organic material was badly decayed before it reached the museum, or once exhibited, became devastated by moth. Jameson was among a group of early nineteenth-century scholars in Europe who were beginning to take a scientific interest in people in other parts of the world and their manners and customs, and collecting artefacts out of a new awareness.

Attitudes towards foreign material culture developed rapidly in the nineteenth century. In 1854 the Director of the newly-formed Industrial Museum of Scotland in Edinburgh, George Wilson, began to implement systematic collecting policies. He used Scots working for the Hudson's Bay Company in Canada as agents and, like Jameson, issued specific collecting requirements. Substantial Arctic and Subarctic collections resulted which are among the earliest systematic documented collections of Canadian ethnography. Much Canadian Indian and Inuit material was brought to Scotland as souvenirs by retiring Bay officials or sent as gifts to friends and relatives, and such objects continue to find their way into Scotland's museums in this century.

George Wilson in Scotland, his brother Daniel in Canada, General Pitt Rivers in England, and other scholars in Europe were part of a new movement of ideas concerning the material culture of other peoples which developed in the late nineteenth century. Technology, including the raw materials, the processes of manufacture and the function of the finished product, began to be of serious interest. George Wilson collected within defined classifications and exhibited in systematic arrangements and, like Pitt Rivers, aimed to instruct in the development of technology, using ordinary and typical specimens which had been selected and arranged in sequence rather than rare objects.

Many public museums emerged in Scotland in the late nineteenth century. This growth was related to new ideas about universal education and coincided with the great Victorian period of the British Empire, in which Scots played a prominent role worldwide. As a consequence foreign material culture, especially from Africa, Asia and the Pacific, found its way in quantity into museums. By the early twentieth century museums all over Scotland held collections of foreign ethnography, although there were no dedicated specialist staff to look after them. These artefacts were often exhibited on the comparative model promoted by Pitt Rivers in his own museums, an influential formula which persisted well into this century.

As British colonial responsibilities have waned, the latter part of the twentieth century has witnessed a general decline in the collecting of foreign ethnography in Scotland. Many museums in the 1960s and 1970s, pursuing policies of local interest in the fields of archaeology, social history and natural history, suppressed foreign ethnography, or transferred collections to other homes. The commercial value of much ethnographic material, especially that regarded as 'art', has escalated since the 1950s and as a consequence fewer objects are given to museums. The inexorable rise in market prices has in turn reduced the number of museums able to purchase material, and even the largest museums have experienced a slowing in collection growth.

Nonetheless, there have been encouraging developments in museums holding collections of foreign ethnography.

The first specialist curator was appointed in Edinburgh in 1964, rapidly followed by ethnography curator posts in Aberdeen (1966) and Glasgow Museums (1976). In addition, both the current director and his predecessor at the University of Glasgow's Hunterian Museum and Art Gallery are eminent African ethnographers. Apart from these posts, the care of foreign ethnographic collections in museums in Scotland rests largely in the hands of curators with wider responsibilities, such as human history, archaeology or applied arts.

A number of museums exhibit ethnographic material. Those with the largest collections, in Edinburgh, Aberdeen, and at Kelvingrove and the Hunterian in Glasgow, have permanent displays of objects. These museums also mount temporary exhibitions based either upon their own material or on loans. In the past decade several museums have taken a fresh look at their collections. The Marischal Museum, University of Aberdeen, with its influential permanent display 'About Human Beings: About Being Human' (1985), is a stimulating example of the intelligent use of a relatively small and uneven collection. This has led the way in Britain for a new style of comparative, cross-cultural ethnographic exhibition which aims to break down the traditional division in museum displays between our own culture and that of others. The McLean Museum and Art Gallery, Greenock, devotes a considerable proportion of exhibition space to ethnographic material from Japan, China, India, Northeast Asia and Oceania. Some of the displays deal with a specific culture in some depth, whilst others aim to show diversity and cross-cultural influences within an area.

Perth Museum and Art Gallery has marked its important and early collection by publishing a catalogue of the African, Pacific and American materials (1983). In a current exhibition 'The Time of Our Lives: An Introduction to the History of a District', Perth includes their rare eighteenth-century Tahitian mourner's costume in the section on Travel and Discovery to underline a little-known aspect of Perth's history. Several other museums use ethnographic objects to document the unusual lives or activities of local people. In Blantyre the David Livingstone Centre incorporates African items in a display illustrating the background and life of Livingstone, while at the Laing Museum in Newburgh objects from Fiji highlight the theme of emigration in an exhibition on the interests and activities of the towns-people in the Victorian period. Nairn Museum, which is run by a local society with volunteer staff, displays African, Pacific and American artefacts collected by local people abroad, and in 1992 presented a commemorative exhibition devoted to James Grant, the explorer.

A few museums in Scotland undertake a limited amount of collecting in the field in order to record non-European societies in the contemporary world. The National Museums of Scotland, as part of a general policy to update the national collections by the acquisition of contemporary material, has in recent years documented and collected twentieth-century crafts in Turkey, Japan, Australia, Polynesia, Nigeria and the American Southwest. Staff of Glasgow Museums have also collected in the field in southern Africa, Israel and Australia.

Although fewer museums now actively purchase items from sources such as dealers and auction houses, new opportunities for acquisition are appearing, for example, in the field of 'tourist art'. Indigenous societies have responded in a variety of ways to the market created by the massive growth in foreign travel. Sometimes traditional forms are adapted, especially by making them smaller, to fit more easily into a suitcase, sometimes new forms, like ashtrays, are created to meet visitor needs. These responses, valuable evidence of social change, are valid additions to museum collections. Within Scotland itself, contemporary culture is rapidly becoming more multi-ethnic. Museums are collecting to record this diversity, to reflect contemporary society to their visitors, and to enhance the collections as an educational resource.

As the world approaches a new millennium, collections of foreign ethnography are assuming new significance. Late twentieth-century media and communications have transformed the experience and interests of the public. The development of mass tourism and long-haul travel and the influence of television, which brings other life-styles into our own homes whether or not we travel, has increased awareness of non-European societies and of the need to preserve the world's cultural heritage in a way that has never happened before. In this context collections of foreign ethnography offer fresh opportunities for development, display and educational activity, and provide a unique resource to enhance our understanding both of others and ourselves.

The Programme

In 1977, the Museum Ethnographers Group started gathering information in a survey of ethnographic collections in the United Kingdom. In 1982, the Scottish Museums Council convened a conference of professional ethnographers, conservators, curators and designers/interpreters to discuss common needs and practices in terms of the care, display and interpretation of foreign ethnographic collections within Scotland. The experiences gained in the early years leading to the *Museum Ethnographers Group Survey of Ethnographic Collections in the United Kingdom, Eire and the Channel Islands: Interim Report* (Schumann, 1986), were invaluable to these discussions. The Museum Ethnographers Group survey identified many museums which had relevant material, but the need for a programme in Scotland to record collections in more detail and to survey their needs and those of the institutions holding them, was apparent and confirmed by the Council's membership.

Studies conducted by the Scottish Museums Council and its partners, such as *A Conservation Survey of Museum Collections in Scotland* (Ramer, 1989) and *A World of Learning: University Collections in Scotland* (Drysdale, 1990) established that, while certain foreign ethnographic collections were well known, well used and well looked after, there were others in need of basic or improved documentation and care. It was also anticipated that there might be collections awaiting 'rediscovery' and in need of assessment. The dearth of professional curators working in Scotland with expertise in ethnographic material was, and continues to be, a threat to the welfare of this irreplaceable archive of material.

To identify and meet these needs more specifically, the Scottish Museums Council in conjunction with the National Museums of Scotland and the University of Glasgow devised a two-year programme with five main aims:

1. To establish the location of foreign ethnographic collections in museums, universities, research institutes and private collections in Scotland.

2. To encourage and coordinate the recording of information about foreign ethnographic collections by in-house museum staff.

3. To record collections or organise recording by other specialists in cases where no professional staff are available to undertake the work.

4. To encourage comparative research on key items and collections for publication.

5. To establish a computerised database for the recorded information and to publish the findings of the survey programme.

The dissemination of findings will be to research workers in the field and to museums and allied institutions for use in their collections management and for public exhibitions or similar purposes.

In 1990, funding for a two-year research programme, operated by a full-time coordinator with a knowledge of ethnographic material, and a part-time assistant, was granted by the Economic and Social Research Council. This is the first such award for a programme of this kind from the Council. Work began on 18 March 1991.

Scope of the Programme

The Programme covers indigenous artefacts from Africa, the Americas, Oceania and Asia. The decision to exclude material from Europe was deliberate. The two-year time-scale of the Programme, the manageability of data, the number of collections and objects involved, and the traditional confinement in scope of ethnography to material from pre-industrial societies were factors in this decision. Numismatics, foreign archaeology and works on paper were also excluded since they are areas of specific expertise or methodology. Their presence in collections has been flagged on the database for future reference.

Given the great range and diversity of artefacts, it could not be expected that any one individual would be conversant with such a breadth of material. The Programme budget therefore included an element for visits by specialist ethnographers to assist with the recording process and to examine significant items.

Programme Plan

The two-year Programme was divided into five main activities:

1. The collection of data about artefacts and collections management from museums and other institutions or individuals, using specially designed forms. Data collection was, where possible, undertaken by museum staff themselves. In cases where no specialist staff were avail-

able, recording was done by the Programme Coordinator or by a specialist ethnographer.

2. Data preparation for input into a desk top computer. Data preparation and research was undertaken by the Programme Coordinator in consultation with the Principal Investigator and with specialist ethnographers.

3. Data entry into a structured database to produce a summary catalogue and a set of cross-referenced indexes. Data input was carried out by the Programme Assistant in consultation with the Programme Coordinator and with guidance from ethnography and computing specialists.

4. Data checking to ensure correct entries was carried out by the Programme Coordinator, by participating institutions where possible, and by specialist advisers.

5. Preparation of the findings of the Programme for subquent publication. Upon completion of data input and editing, participant museums received copies of their records as hard-copy printout or on computer disk as appropriate. Disk copies will be available on request to museums which computerise their records in the future.

A more detailed timetable of the Programme is presented in Figure 1.

Figure 1 (*below*): Programme Timetable

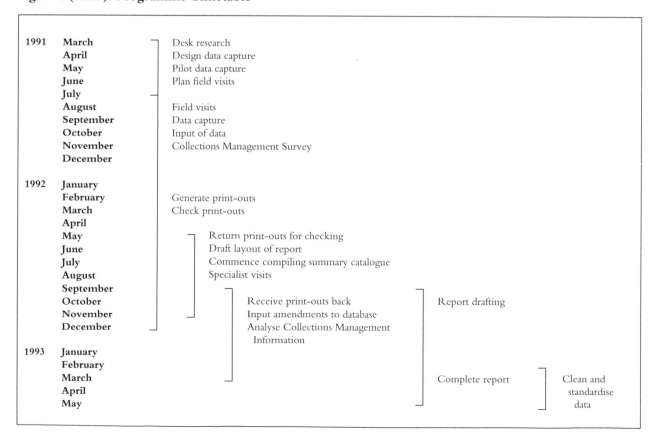

Figure 2 (*opposite*):
Collections Management Proforma

Scottish Museums Council

SURVEY OF FOREIGN ETHNOGRAPHIC COLLECTIONS: COLLECTIONS MANAGEMENT

	Field	Number of characters	Comment (free-text field-notes, not on database)
1	Museum name	10	
2	Location (within the museum)	30	
3	Designated staff for the collection	1	
4	Staff in charge of collection	20	
5	Collection history	200	
6	Transfer details	100	
7	Does collection policy include ethno material	1	
8	Does collection policy include acquisition/disposal	1	
9	Acquisition budget	1	
10	Budget for maintenance	1	
11	Ethno collection used as educational resource	1	
12	Ethno collection used in research	1	
13	Ethno collection used for display	1	
14	Ethno collection used for in-house exhibitions	1	
15	Ethno collection used for external exhibitions	1	
16	Enquiries about ethno collection	1	
17	Public access to ethno collection	1	
18	Environment condition (store)	1	
19	Lighting condition (store)	1	
20	Cleanliness (store)	1	
21	General storage condition	1	
22	General condition of ethno collection	50	
23	Any concerns	100	
24	% Documented	3	
25	Future plans	100	
26	Deaccession considered	1	
27	Transfer considered	1	
28	Number of specimens	5	
29	Numismatics flag	1	
30	Foreign archaeology flag	1	

The Programme Coordinator was appointed and advised by the Foreign Ethnographic Collections Research Programme Management Committee, under the Chairmanship of Professor Frank Willett, formerly Director of the Hunterian Museum and Art Gallery, University of Glasgow, and an authority on West African ethnography and archaeology. Day-to-day support was provided by the Principal Investigator, Dale Idiens, Depute Director (Collections) and Keeper of the Department of History and Applied Art at the National Museums of Scotland, and Timothy Ambrose, Director of the Scottish Museums Council.

In addition to creating a national database of foreign ethnographic collections, a basic survey of collections management issues was also undertaken to establish areas of need which the Scottish Museums Council, museums and their governing bodies, and other interested parties might address.

The survey addressed five main issues:

1 The museum's policy in respect of foreign ethnographic material in its care.

2 The uses to which the museum puts its collections.

3 Staffing of collections.

4 Plans for the future use of the collection.

5 Physical care of the collections.

Where possible, the issues were discussed during a recording visit using a proforma questionnaire (Figure 2), otherwise in writing or by telephone. In many cases, more than one member of staff in the museum was approached. Use was also made of existing information gathered by the Scottish Museums Council's Conservation Service staff.

The purpose of this survey was thus to identify which museums had foreign ethnographic material and to provide the Scottish Museums Council with detailed information on each museum's specific needs in this respect.

Implementation

In order to plan the field visits it was first necessary to identify those museums, institutions or private individuals holding material relevant to the Programme and to ascertain the level of existing documentation and the availability of staff or specialists. Using the Scottish Museums Council's membership as a starting point, institutions and private individuals were invited by letter to participate in the Programme.

Once responses were received, curators and owners were invited to attend a workshop, kindly hosted by the Smith Museum and Art Gallery in Stirling. The aims of the workshop were:

1 To introduce the Programme, its background and context and encourage in participants a sense of ownership of the survey and the database which it was intended to create. Early, personal contact between the participants and the Programme Coordinator was regarded as important.

2 To introduce a range of artefacts to assist participants in recognising material as foreign ethnography. The two specialists leading this session had no prior sight of the objects or related documentation since the aim was to illustrate how to look at material from 'first principles', as the majority of curators must do with foreign ethnography.

3 To introduce participants to ways of using collections and individual objects within a museum context. As a case study, the Curator of the McLean Museum and Art Gallery in Greenock, a geologist by training, explained how the museum had utilised foreign ethnographic material within a major renewal project.

A series of field visits commenced in July 1991 with visits to the Shetland Islands, Orkney and the northernmost parts of the country. In general, the more distant museums were visited first to avoid the delays likely when travelling in Scotland in winter.

The methods of data collection and inputting had to be very flexible as no one museum was identical to another in the organisation or documentation of the collections. It was decided at the outset that, in the absence of a standard terminology and considering the time involved in having constantly to refer to one in the field, terminology would be more easily regulated retrospectively, once the material was on the database and accessible for global editing.

For large collections and collections already adequately documented the information was transferred to Edinburgh to input directly. This was generally done by providing photocopies, although in a few cases, and subject to strict security conditions, original documentation was lent for inputting. However, the majority of collections lacked adequate documentation and in these cases a proforma recording sheet was completed by the Programme Coordinator for each item or group of items during a site visit (Figure 3).

Figure 3 (*opposite*): Proforma Object Record

Scottish Museums Council

SURVEY OF FOREIGN ETHNOGRAPHIC COLLECTIONS: OBJECT RECORD

	Field	Number of characters	Comment (free-text field-notes)
1	Museum name	10	
2	Identification number	15	
3	Previous number	20	
4	Object name	64	
5	Number of items	4	
6	Original description	254	
7	Physical description	254	
8	Dimensions	24	
9	Associated name	50	
10	Date of association	40	
11	Country / continent	20	
12	Region	20	
13	District	20	
14	Place	50	
15	Original geographical location	30	
16	Culture / people	64	
17	Date of manufacture	50	
18	Source name	50	
19	Source role	15	
20	Acquisition method	1	
21	Acquisition year	4	
22	Current location	20	
23	Bibliography	1	
24	Recorder	10	
25	Date of recording	8	
26	ISN	5	
27	Record OK flag	1	
28	Inspect object flag	1	
29	Suggested specialist	1	
20	Human remains flag	1	
31	Record notes	254	

Staff and Equipment

The completion of the proforma was a time-consuming process unless assisted by a member of the museum staff. For two collections in particular where staff were available to assist the Coordinator in the location, recording and relocation of material, basic improvements were brought about in the level of documentation and storage conditions. Where no assistance was available, a micro-tape recorder was used. The tape recorder was useful in situations where access to objects was difficult or where the number of objects had been underestimated in relation to the time allocated. A compact camera with built-in optional flash, telephoto and wide-angle facilities proved an invaluable tool. A torch was also useful.

Health and safety aspects of working with museum collections, particularly ethnographic material, have never been fully explored. In addition to artefact-related hazards such as rusted metal, animal products (dried blood, feathers, skin, etc), and the risk from 'poisoned arrows', there are many hazards arising out of poor environmental conditions, inaccessible or unsafe storage, unsafe buildings, vermin droppings, dirt and dust. Cotton gloves were worn to protect objects but disposable surgical gloves proved more practical. Disposable 'Tyvek' cover-alls with elasticated wrist and ankle cuffs and hood, disposable dust masks and a warm cotton boiler-suit for particularly cold environments were necessary. The use of low-cost disposable protective clothing offered some protection, lowered the risk of carrying insect life between museums and reduced laundry requirements when travelling. A basic first-aid kit also proved necessary. The *Control of Substances Hazardous to Health* Regulations (1988) are referred to in more detail on page 66.

Case-study: Paisley Museum and Art Galleries

During the field recording process itself, a number of practical and valuable outcomes were achieved. A case-study of Paisley Museum serves to illustrate the benefits of working with a member of the museum staff to both the Programme and the collection.

The collection consisted of approximately 1500 items, 1000 of which bore no accession number or had only an original page number from an old ledger. The collection was stored in a former Army Barracks building in which some rooms had been fitted out with steel shelving but which otherwise retained the original fittings, wallpaper and floor coverings.

The shelves in the storage areas were allocated a number and material was removed item by item, allocated a number if necessary, and recorded. When one shelf was completed, suitable material was boxed and the number marked, along with other contents, in indelible pen on the side of each box so as to be visible when stacked.

Such was the amount of material that the time originally allocated was inadequate and a second visit had to be arranged a few months later. The intervening period was put to good use by the Museums Service's Collections Manager. With the assistance of the Museum Registrar, the Collections Manager checked through the original ledgers and accession records using the object name and description allocated by the Programme Coordinator and linked a large percentage of the items to the original entries, confirming or correcting provenances, eliciting donors, source, and history. In cases where the original accession number was rediscovered, the allocated working number was moved to the previous number field on the record. As a result, some 60 per cent of the items were reunited with their original entry details. On the second visit a similar procedure was followed.

The Programme Coordinator, with the agreement of the Museums Service's Chief Officer and the Collections Manager, arranged for the Scottish Museums Council Conservation Services Manager to visit and recommend some basic, low-cost environmental improvements. These recommendations were well received and effected the sealing of two open fireplaces as an anti-dust measure and the temporary screening of two windows to reduce light. To reduce dust further, it was suggested that the room be redecorated and the shelving curtained with 'Tyvek' sheeting. At the time of writing most of these recommendations have been implemented.

The collection contains a large number of items of nineteenth-century date from south-east Nigeria, particularly the Cross River area. Keith Nicklin, Keeper of Ethnography at the Horniman Museum in London, and Jill Salmons, Lecturer in Art History at Worcester College of Technology, were invited to Paisley to look at this material and give the benefit of their specialist expertise.

The allocation of numbers to objects, the locating of objects on numbered shelves and the collating of original information available on individual record sheets and printouts enabled, probably for the first time, the serious consideration of the material in ethnographic and museum terms. The specialists were able to add significantly to the information about the objects in a more effective manner than would have been possible previously.

What was an undocumented collection considered to be of little importance has been documented, partially restored in improved conditions and is now known to be of some significance. It is hoped that as a result of the Programme, its future may be reviewed.

Participant Museums

The number in the left-hand margin refers to the map of the distribution of collections in Scotland (page 16).

1   Abbotsford
Melrose
Roxburghshire TD6 9BQ

2   Aberdeen Art Gallery and Museums
Art Gallery
Schoolhill
Aberdeen AB9 1FQ

3   Andrew Carnegie Birthplace Museum
Moodie Street
Dunfermline
Fife KY12 7PL

4   Angus District Museums
Montrose Museum and Art Gallery
Panmure Place
Montrose DD10 8HE

5   The Argyll and Sutherland Highlanders
Regimental Museum
The Castle
Stirling FK8 1EH

6   The Black Watch Museum
Balhousie Castle
Hay Street
Perth PH1 5HR

7   The Cameronians (Scottish Rifles) Regimental
Museum
Mote Hill
Off Muir Street
Hamilton ML3 6BY

8   Museum of Childhood (Branch of: Edinburgh
City Museums and Art Galleries)
42 High Street
Edinburgh EH1 1TG

9   City Art Centre (Branch of: Edinburgh City
Museums and Art Galleries)
2 Market Street
Edinburgh EH1 1DE

10   Cunninghame District Council Museums
Service
10 Glasgow Vennel
Irvine KA12 0BD

11   The David Livingstone Centre
Blantyre
Glasgow G72 9BT

12   The Dick Institute
Elmbank Avenue
Kilmarnock KA1 3BU

13   Dumfries Museum
The Observatory
Church Street
Dumfries DG2 7SW

14   Dundee Art Galleries and Museums
McManus Galleries
Albert Square
Dundee DD1 1DA

15   Dunrobin Castle
Golspie
Sutherland KW10 2SF
         Correspondence to:
         Sutherland Estates
         Golspie
         Sutherland KW10 6RP

16   Elgin Museum
1 High Street
Elgin IV30 1EQ

17   Edinburgh University Collection of Historic
Musical Instruments
Reid Concert Hall
Bristo Square
Edinburgh EH8 9AG

18   Ettrick and Lauderdale District Museums
          Service
      Municipal Buildings
      High Street
      Selkirk TD7 4JX

19   Falconer Museum
      Tolbooth Street
      Forres
      Moray IV36 0PH

20   Fochabers Folk Museum
      Pringle Antiques
      High Street
      Fochabers
      Moray IV32 7DU
              Correspondence to: Christies
                 (Fochabers) Ltd
              The Nurseries
              Fochabers
              Moray IV32 7PF

21   Glasgow Museums
      Kelvingrove
      Glasgow G3 8AG

22   Hawick Museum
      Wilton Lodge Park
      Hawick
      Roxburghshire TD9 7JL

23   Hunterian Museum and Art Gallery
      University of Glasgow
      Glasgow G12 8QQ

24   Inverness Museum and Art Gallery
      Castle Wynd
      Inverness IV2 3ED

25   John Hastie Museum
      Threestanes Road
      Strathaven ML10 6DX
              Correspondence to:
              Central Library
              East Kilbride G74 1PG

26   Kelburne Castle Museum
      Fairlie
      Ayrshire KA29 0BE

27   Kirkcaldy Museum and Art Gallery
      War Memorial Gardens
      Kirkcaldy
      Fife KY1 1YG

28   Lhaidhay Croft Museum
      Dunbeath
      Caithness KW6 6EH

29   McLean Museum and Art Gallery
      15 Kelly Street
      Greenock PA16 8JX

30   MacRobert Arts Centre Galleries
      MacRobert Arts Centre
      University of Stirling
      Stirling FK9 4LA

31   Marischal Museum
      Marischal College
      University of Aberdeen
      Aberdeen AB9 1AS

32   Monklands District Council Museums
              Correspondence to: The Chief
                 Librarian
              Academy Street
              Coatbridge ML5 3AW

33   Mull Museum
      Main Street
      Tobermory
      Isle of Mull
      Argyll PA75 6NY

34   Nairn Literary Institute Museum
      Viewfield House
      Nairn

35   National Museums of Scotland
      Chambers Street
      Edinburgh EH1 1JF

36   The National Trust for Scotland
          (Collections located in various properties)
      5 Charlotte Square
      Edinburgh EH2 4DU

37   North Berwick Museum
      School Road
      North Berwick
      East Lothian
              Correspondence to:
              East Lothian District Museums Service
              Library HQ, Lodge Street
              Haddington EH41 3DX

38   North East Fife District Museum Service
      County Buildings
      Cupar
      Fife KY15 4TA
              Displays located at:
              Laing Museum
              High Street
              Newburgh
              Fife KY14 6DX

| 39 | North East of Scotland Museums Service
Arbuthnot Museum
St Peter Street
Peterhead AB42 6QD |
| 40 | Paisley Museum and Art Galleries
High Street
Paisley PA1 2BA |
| 41 | Perth Museum and Art Gallery
George Street
Perth PH1 5LB |
| 42 | The Royal Scots Regimental Museum
The Castle
Edinburgh EH1 2YT |
| 43 | The Rozelle Galleries
Kyle and Carrick District Libraries and
    Museums
Rozelle Park
Monument Road
Alloway
Ayr KA7 4NQ |
| 44 | University of St Andrews
Department of Museum Studies
College Gate
North Street
St Andrews KY16 7AJ |
| 45 | Shetland Museum
Lower Hillhead
Lerwick ZE1 0EL |
| 46 | The Stewartry Museum
St Mary Street
Kirkcudbright DG6 4AQ |
| 47 | Smith Art Gallery and Museum
40 Albert Place
Dumbarton Road
Stirling FK8 2RQ |
| 48 | Strathkelvin District Museums
The Cross
Kirkintilloch
Glasgow G66 1AB |
| 49 | Stromness Museum
52 Alfred Street
Stromness
Orkney KW16 3DF |
| 50 | Tain Museum
Castle Brae
Tain
Ross-shire IV19 1AJ |

51   Tweeddale Museum
      Chambers Institute
      High Street
      Peebles EH45 8AP

52   Wick Heritage Centre
      19-27 Bank Row
      Wick
      Caithness KW1 5EY

53   Wigtown Museum
      Town Hall
      Main Street
      Wigtown
              Correspondence to:
              Stranraer Museum
              The Old Town Hall
              George Street
              Stranraer DG9 7JP

The Distribution of Museums

The pattern which emerges on the map from this plot of museums holding foreign ethnographic material reflects the distribution of museums as a whole in Scotland. Scotland's museums inevitably follow the pattern of population development and the majority are spread across the central belt of the country, weighted at each end by Glasgow and Edinburgh with Stirling slightly to the north. Between the two principal sites there is a scatter of museums near the west coast and in Ayrshire, to the south of Glasgow. The concentration of collections in this central belt may reflect the concentration of heavy industry in the area.

Another notable feature is the line of museums along the east coast of Scotland, a distribution established through maritime activity from the Firth of Forth and Edinburgh around the coast of Fife to the River Tay and Perth, through Dundee, and continuing up the coast northwards to Orkney and Shetland. There is also a cluster of museums centred around Hawick in the Borders, relating to the growth in population associated with nineteenth-century weaving industries.

Museums in Scotland (HMSO, 1986), known more commonly as the 'Miles Report', gives a useful background to Scotland's museums, including an analysis of their distribution.

The Distribution of Museums in Scotland with Collections of Foreign Ethnography

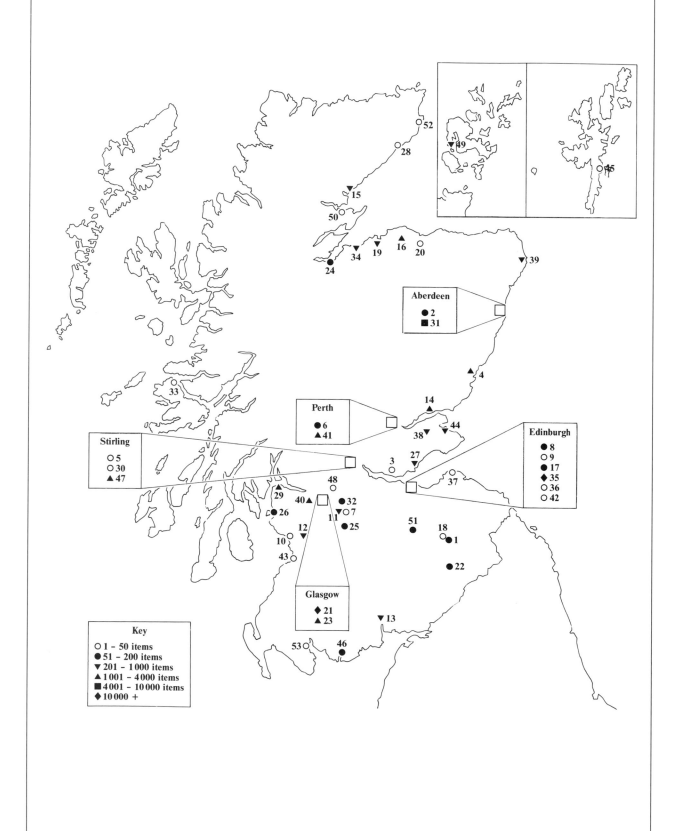

Aberdeen
- ● 2
- ■ 31

Perth
- ● 6
- ▲ 41

Stirling
- ○ 5
- ○ 30
- ▲ 47

Edinburgh
- ● 8
- ○ 9
- ● 17
- ◆ 35
- ○ 36
- ○ 42

Glasgow
- ◆ 21
- ▲ 23

Key
- ○ 1 – 50 items
- ● 51 – 200 items
- ▼ 201 – 1000 items
- ▲ 1001 – 4000 items
- ■ 4001 – 10 000 items
- ◆ 10 000 +

Number of objects in museums surveyed

Museum	No of objects	Map number
National Museums of Scotland [N]	39022	35
Glasgow Museums (Kelvingrove & Burrell) [LA]	14000	21
Marischal Museum, Aberdeen [U]	9590	31
Perth Museum and Art Gallery [LA]	3162	41
Hunterian Museum and Art Gallery, Glasgow [U]	2928	23
Smith Art Gallery and Museum, Stirling [I]	2808	47
Dundee Art Galleries and Museums [LA]	2680	14
Paisley Museum and Art Galleries [LA]	1538	40
Angus District Museums [LA]	1290	4
McLean Museum and Art Gallery, Greenock [LA]	1267	29
Elgin Museum [I]	1240	16
The Dick Institute, Kilmarnock [LA]	990	12
The David Livingstone Centre, Blantyre [I]	725	11
North East of Scotland Museums Service [LA]	717	39
Dunrobin Castle Museum, Golspie [P]	698	15
Falconer Museum, Forres [LA]	562	19
North East Fife District Museum Service [LA]	415	38
Dumfries Museum [LA]	413	13
Kirkcaldy Museum and Art Gallery [LA]	334	27
Nairn Literary Institute Museum [I]	312	34
Stromness Museum, Orkney [I]	249	49
Aberdeen Art Gallery and Museums [LA]	209	2
University of St Andrews [U]	202	44
Hawick Museum [LA]	192	22
Monklands District Council Museums, Coatbridge [LA]	160	32
Tweeddale Museum, Peebles [LA]	154	51
Abbotsford, Melrose [P]	146	1
Edinburgh University Collection of Historic Musical Instruments [U]	143	17
Museum of Childhood, Edinburgh [LA]	130	8
The Black Watch Museum, Perth [R]	77	6

Museum	No of Objects	Map number
Inverness Museum and Art Gallery [LA]	74	24
Kelburne Castle Museum, Fairlie [P]	66	26
The Stewartry Museum, Kircudbright [LA]	63	46
John Hastie Museum, Strathaven [LA]	58	25
Cunninghame District Council Museums Service [LA]	45	10
The Cameronians (Scottish Rifles) Regimental Museum, Hamilton [R]	42	7
The Argyll and Sutherland Highlanders Regimental Museum, Stirling [R]	35	5
The Rozelle Galleries, Alloway [I/LA]	31	43
Shetland Museum [LA]	25	45
The Royal Scots Regimental Museum, Edinburgh [R]	19	42
Strathkelvin District Museums, Kirkintilloch [LA]	15	48
North Berwick Museum [LA]	15	37
The National Trust for Scotland [I]	15	36
Andrew Carnegie Birthplace Museum, Dunfermline [I]	14	3
Wigtown Museum [LA]	8	53
Tain Museum [I]	8	50
Fochabers Folk Museum [P]	6	20
Wick Heritage Centre [I]	4	52
Ettrick and Lauderdale District Museums Service, Selkirk [LA]	3	18
City Art Centre, Edinburgh [LA]	1	9
Lhaidhay Croft Museum, Dunbeath [LA]	1	28
MacRobert Arts Centre and Gallery, Stirling [U]	1	30
Mull Museum, Tobermory [I]	1	33

Total number of objects 86649

Number of museums surveyed 53

Number of museums by managing authority:

[LA]	Local Authority Museum	28
[I]	Independent Museum	11
[U]	University Collection or Museum	5
[P]	Private Collection or Museum	4
[R]	Regimental Collection or Museum	4
[N]	National Museum	1

PART II:
THE FOREIGN
ETHNOGRAPHIC
COLLECTIONS
NATIONAL
DATABASE

The National Database

Ian O Morrison

Design

The Foreign Ethnographic Collections Research
Programme database structure was designed to be
compatible with the system used for recording foreign
ethnographic material in the National Museums of
Scotland. Additional fields were included to cope with
the specific requirements of the survey, such as indicating
the need for an object to be examined by a specialist.

The fields used for data entry were as follows:

Field Name	Number of Characters	Description
MUSEUM	10	Name of museum or institution
IDENTN	15	Accession/identifying number
OBJNME	64	Simple name for object(s)
OBJITM	4	Number of objects in group
ORDESC	254	Original description from catalogue cards, labels, registers etc
DIMNSN	24	Dimensions
PHDESC	254	Physical description, including materials
DSPDAT	50	Date of object
REGION	20	Broad area of origin (e.g. continent)
COUNTRY	20	Narrower area of origin (e.g. country)
DISTRICT	20	Even narrower area of origin (e.g. district)
PLACE	50	Narrowest area of origin
CULTURE	64	Culture or people(s) associated with the object
ANDISP	50	Collector or other associated person
ANREL	32	Nature of association
ACQYY	4	Year of acquisition by museum
SRCNME	50	Name of donor/lender/vendor
SRCROL	15	Role of source (donor/lender/vendor etc)
METHOD	1	Method of acquisition ("D"= donation,"L"= loan, etc)
CLOC	20	Current location of object
PRVNUM	20	Previous identifying numbers
BIBLIOG	1	Bibliographic references
RECORDER	4	Recorder initials
DATE	8	Date of recording
ISN	5	Internal Serial Number (computer-generated)
FLAGOK	1	Record OK flag (Y/N). Indicates whether or not record is suspect
FLAGINSPCT	1	Is a further opinion needed?
SPECIALIST	20	Suggested specialist
HUMAN	1	Does the item constitute or include human remains?
NOTES	250	Any other information
GEONAR	50	Original geographical name

The Applications

The data entry application was written to maximise efficiency in recording information about the objects surveyed. It was written in *Clipper* by Ian Morrison, Scottish Museums Documentation Officer at the National Museums of Scotland. *Clipper* is a widely used application development programming language which produces standard dBase-compatible files. The application will run on any IBM-compatible PC with a hard disk and also provides basic retrieval facilities, including the ability to print individual records and listings.

The database has now been transferred to the National Museums of Scotland computer system where it is accessed through *Minisis* software. This offers flexible querying and a closer relationship with the National Museums' record of its own ethnographic holdings.

Access and Retrieval

The National Museums of Scotland will hold the computerised database in the care of the Scottish Museums Documentation Officer and it is expected that the National Museums of Scotland will be the home of the database in the long term. Access to the information already on the database is available to the museums providing the information and to researchers.

Pan-Scottish queries, such as those in the sample below, can be answered directly by staff at the National Museums of Scotland. Queries relating to individual museum collections will be dealt with by staff in the museums concerned and should be directed to them. Addresses of participant museums may be found in this report and in the Museums Association *Museum Yearbook*.

It is possible to supply sections of the database, together with the original application on floppy disk, or as printout. Distribution of information in this way will take place only where there is written permission from the museum whose collection is concerned. It is the responsibility of the enquirer to obtain this permission and forward it to the National Museums of Scotland.

Sample queries for the National Database

Which Scottish museums have objects from Western Australia ? Angus District Museums, Glasgow Museums, Hunterian Museum and Art Gallery, Marischal Museum, National Museums of Scotland, Perth Museum and Art Gallery, Stewartry Museum.

Do any Scottish museums have objects collected by Constance F Gordon Cumming ? Yes - the Falconer Museum and the National Museums of Scotland.

Do any Scottish museums have non-European canoes? There are twenty complete, full-size canoes. Many museums have examples of paddles, parts of canoes, and model canoes.

Which Scottish museums have Maori objects? Angus District Museums, Dundee Art Galleries and Museums, Elgin Museum, Glasgow Museums, Hunterian Museum and Art Gallery, Kirkcaldy Museum and Art Gallery, Marischal Museum, North East Fife District Museum Service, National Museums of Scotland, The National Trust for Scotland, Paisley Museum and Art Galleries, Perth Museum and Art Gallery, Smith Art Gallery and Museum, the Stewartry Museum, Wigtown Museum.

More detailed queries should be directed to the individual museums concerned.

The database can also be searched for free-text. This means that any word or combination of words may be used as the basis for a search. For example:

I am doing a survey of indigenous use of feathers. Which museums have objects which have *feathers* included in them?
Search for the word *feathers*.

Does any Scottish museum have an item which includes *moss*?
Search for the word *moss*.

Are there any examples of *woven palm-leaf* in Scottish museums?
Search for the words in the phrase *woven palm-leaf* as a group, individually, or in any combination of the three elements.

The implications for using the database for research other than that directly related to foreign ethnography, such as Natural History or Textile Design, are clear. For instance, researchers enquiring into indigenous use of materials in the geographical and cultural areas covered by the Foreign Ethnographic Collections National Database will find the database useful.

Upgrading

The National Museums of Scotland welcome initiatives to improve the accuracy and completeness of the database. Participant museums wishing to make alterations and additions to the database should contact the Scottish Museums Documentation Officer to agree the format in which the data should be passed to the National Museums of Scotland.

National Databases Containing Information from Collections Research Projects

1. The National Museums of Scotland hold databases containing records from the following collections research projects which have been carried out in collaboration with the Scottish Museums Council:

> Natural Sciences Collections Research Unit
> Industrial Heritage Scotland
> Foreign Ethnographic Collections Research Programme.

It is likely that further projects will be undertaken.

2. The National Museums of Scotland provide the technical support for database compilation and maintenance. In particular, the Scottish Museums Documentation Officer prepares application software which can be used to compile, edit and search databases, and gives advice on the use of software, hardware, methods and standardisation.

3. The National Museums of Scotland are responsible for making the data available as appropriate and also give long-term security to the databases.

4. It is the responsibility of interest groups in various curatorial disciplines to collect, input and edit data. These groups establish collections research projects to gather information.

5. The provision of the information, its upgrading and improvement is the responsibility of the individual museums.

Sample objects from the National Database

The illustrations on pages 24 to 39 show a small selection of objects from collections of foreign ethnography in Scotland. Each photograph is accompanied by the object record as held on the National Database in May 1993.

Accession : **KILMARNOCK E596**	No. : **1**

Name : **Figure**

Original Description :

Physical Description :
Carved wood female with infant on back, seated on stool, headrest, necklace, scarification. Ekwotame funerary figure.

Period :	Dim. : **H.710mm**

Place names : **W. Africa**   **Nigeria**
Benue

Culture : **Idoma**

Assoc. Name :

Association :

Source :

Role :	Method :
Location :	Previous :

Notes :
Ekwotame attribution by Nicklin, 1992.

Flags : **IMPORTANT**	

Ethnography Survey   ISN:4232
EIK   23/10/1991

Accession : DUNDEE	1913.137-106	No. : 1

Name : Figure

Original Description :
Cat card: 2 antique bronzes from ruins of King's Palace.

Physical Description :
Dated to c.17th century.(Sword on reverse of 3 figure piece = maker's mark?)Figure of a warrior from an altar piece. 1) is a figure of a warrior from just above the knees, a very elaborate sculpture. 2) is D shaped pendant representing oba & attendants

Period : probably 17th century	Dim. : 105x102x161

Place names : **Nigeria**
Benin city

Culture :

Assoc. Name :

Association :

Source : **Rattray, P, Dr**

Role : donor	Method : donation
Location : MCM/S3/16/TR37 1989	Previous : case 39/222-223

Notes :
GK:1984. Seen by Frank Willett, 26/6/92

Flags : **FW TO INSPECT |IMPORTANT |**

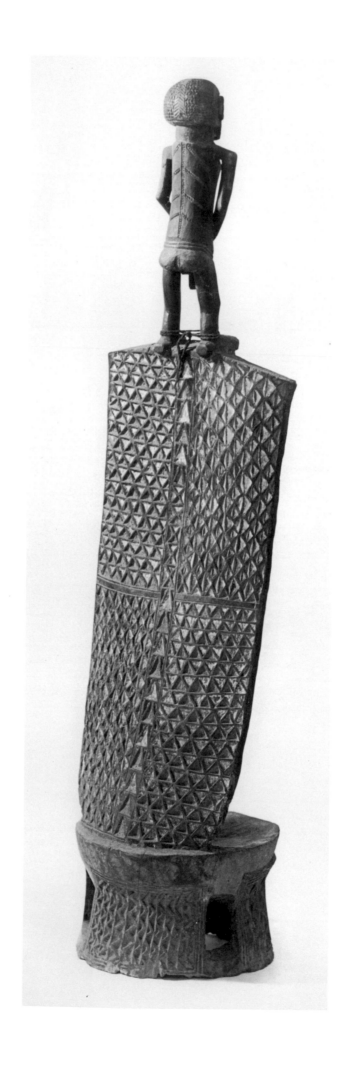

Accession : **NEFMS**	**1981.5**	No. : **1**

Name : Throne

Original Description :

Physical Description :
Wood & polychrome decoration on rear.

Period :	Dim. : **H.1510mm**

Place names : **Zambia**

Culture : **Tabwa**

Assoc. Name : **Young, Robert A**

Association :

Source : **Young,Robert A**

Role : **donor**	Method : **gift**
Location : **1/bw8&9**	Previous :

Notes :

Flags : **IMPORTANT** |

Accession : **McLEAN** **1981.859**	No. : **1**

Name : **Hat**

Original Description :

Physical Description :
Basketry hat (woman's) with black, cream and quill/basketry.
Warp prob. of hazel shoots, weft of split conifer root.
Decorated with half twist overlay and pattern of zig-zag type
in light and dark tan and black. Worn by women.

Period :	Dim. : **HEIGHT:95mm DIAM. 184mm**

Place names : **N. America   California/S Oregon**

Culture : **Yurok**

Assoc. Name :

Association :

Source : **Miss Boyd**

Role : **Donor**	Method : **donation 1912**
Location :	Previous :

Notes :
Yurok attribution by DI 1992

Flags : **IMPORTANT |**

Accession : PMAGx 3156	No. : 1

Name : Figure

Original Description :
"Daikoko, god of Plenty, stoneware"

Physical Description :
Japanese, stoneware. Daikoku, one of 7 gods of good luck. God of wealth and riches. Kiln mark on back. Bizen Kiln ? Sitting on rice bale with rice malette. Script on back. Shoulder with monor damage.

Period : **pre 1935**	Dim. : **H.503mm W.285mm D.206mm**

Place names : **Japan**
                    Bizen

Culture :

Assoc. Name :

Association :

Source : **MacGregor, John**

Role : **donor**	Method : **donation**
Location :	Previous :

Notes :
Attribution confirmed by Jane Wilkinson, 1992. Restoration to be encouraged.

Flags : **IMPORTANT |**

Ethnography Survey
EK   17/01/1992   ISN:6200

Accession : HAWICK	N/N	No. : 1

Name : Clock

Original Description :
Japanese clock 400 years old

Physical Description :
Glass case on wooden trapezium base. Brass mechanism. Store
weights. Ropes. Lantern clock. Double foliot system.

Period : 18th Century? (mid-Edo	Dim. : H.1470mm

Place names : Japan

Culture :

Assoc. Name :

Association :

Source : Wilson, George H

Role : donor	Method : donation 1910
Location : Store	Previous : 10/1

Notes :
'It is an example of the double foliot system to surmount the
problem of indicating the unequal hours of daylight and
darkness and the clock is switched from one to the other at the
appropriate time automatically by the striking the train.

Flags : David Thompson, BM TO INSPECT |IMPORTANT |

Accession : MARISCHAL 531A	No. : 1

Name : Pudding plate

Original Description :
cat card: Pudding plate, Chief's, wooden, oval, decorative
handles - one with raised stylised head in centre of open,
oval, serrated fish-tail end; other handle mounted with similar
head, but face broken away.

Physical Description :
cat card cont: Illustrated on page 13 of photographic Album
(slip cat. no 531A) compiled by the Rev F G Bowie, of the New
Hebrides Group. without handles L.715mm, with handles L.1214mm
Widest B. 290mm

Period : pre 1974	Dim. : 1214mm

Place names : New Hebrides	SW Santo ?

Culture :

Assoc. Name : Bowie

Association :

Source : Bowie, F J T

Role : presented by	Method : 1974

Location :	Previous :

Notes :
See also No.53. (Mrs FJT Bowie is the daughter-in-law of the
Rev FG Bowie, MA, & widow of Dr FJT Bowie).

Flags :

Ethnography Survey   ISN:10314
     24/03/1992

Accession : **Paisley** **1941.6e**	No. : **1**

Name : **Canoe prow ornament.**

Original Description :
Carved wooden idol

Physical Description :

Period : **Late 19th Century**	Dim. : **L.445mm H.290mm**

Place names : **Marquesas Islands**

Magdalena

Culture :

Assoc. Name :

Association :

Source : **Gow, L**

Role : **donor**	Method : **donation**
Location : **U14**	Previous :

Notes :
Attribution by DI 1984

Flags : **IMPORTANT** |

Introduction to the Summary Catalogue

One of the principal objectives of the Foreign Ethnographic Collections Research Programme has been the creation of a computerised National Database of foreign ethnographic material in Scotland. The summary catalogue presented here has been compiled from this database to present an overview of the geographical provenances and major donors of the material. It shows the occurrence of material in broad geographical categories, the Scottish museums in which the material is to be found, and the number of items from that category in each museum.

The summary catalogue acts as an aid to the use of the National Database, which holds the detailed object records and is held and managed by the National Museums of Scotland. Object records from the database caption the illustrations in this publication.

How to use the Summary Catalogue

To assist in the use of the summary catalogue two place-name guides are provided, neither of which is exhaustive. *Place-name Guide 1* is an alphabetical list of place-names indicating which broad geographical heading each place-name is found under in the summary catalogue. *Place-name Guide 2* is a list of broad geographical headings indicating which place-names are included under each heading, providing a cross-reference to *Place-name Guide 1*. In the Summary Catalogue those items which have not been identified beyond a broad geographical heading are listed at the beginning of each continental category. It is hoped that as experts come to study these items in the future, more specific provenances may be added to the database record by the individual museum concerned. Information on how museums may update or amend their records on the database is given on page 22.

Source and associated names

The records held on the National Database give names of donors of items where known and also names of people who are associated with items but are not necessarily the donors. For example, material collected on the voyages of Captain James Cook may have been donated by Captain King. Cook would therefore appear in the associated name field and King in the donor field. Donor significance may be within the context of the museum or nationally, and relate to the number of objects associated with the donor or reflect the donor's historical significance in his or her own right.

Names of particular note are: Dr W B Baikie, RN; Sir Thomas Brisbane; Sir William Burrell; H G Beasley (appearing in record as Cranmore Ethnographical Museum); Frederick W Beechey; Isabella Bird; J Y Buchanan; Sir D Y Cameron; Captain James Cook; J H Dixon or Dickson; Henry Dyer; Capt J Falconer; Sir Arthur Gordon; Constance F Gordon Cumming; Professor J W Gregory; E A Hornell; Capt King; Alexander Laing; Dr David Livingstone; The Rt Hon Sir W Macgregor; Guy Massie-Taylor; Dr N Gordon Munro; William E Parry; Major P H G Powell-Cotton; Dr John Rae; Dr Peter Rattray; Sir Herbert Read; Colin Robertson; Mary Slessor; H W Seton Kerr; Robert Louis Stevenson; Olive Temple; Sir Everard im Thurn.

There are many interesting and unusual objects in collections of foreign ethnography in Scotland. The photographs in this publication illustrate just a few, and others are described in the articles cited in Appendix 3. All objects of foreign ethnography are of interest in some way, but there are some items which, because of their rarity, quality, material, age, or association, are regarded as being of particular significance. Examples include a nineteenth-century carved and painted wooden throne from the Tabwa people of East Africa in the collections of North East Fife District Museum Service; a Pre-Columbian stone belt from the Antilles in the Marischal Museum and an eighteenth-century Maori 'kakapo' feather cloak in Perth Museum and Art Gallery.

The Foreign Ethnographic Collections Research Programme has established that the largest proportion of all foreign ethnography in Scotland is Asian in origin. There is, for example, important Chinese and Japanese material in Aberdeen Art Galleries and Museums, the Marischal Museum, Dundee Art Galleries and Museums, Glasgow Museums, Perth Museum and Art Gallery, Paisley Museum and Art Galleries, the McLean Museum and Art Gallery, Greenock, and the National Museums of Scotland in Edinburgh. The National Museums have a remarkable collection of early Chinese lacquer, while in Glasgow Museums there is a collection of Japanese material given by the Japanese Government in 1878 which is of considerable historical significance. Glasgow Museums also have important Turkish, Iranian and Indo-Iranian carpets. There is early material from Tibet in the Marischal Museum and the National Museums of Scotland.

Objects from Africa form the next largest group in

Scottish collections and material is again widespread with, for example, important Benin metalwork from Nigeria in Dundee, Glasgow and Edinburgh.

Pacific material forms the third group in terms of quantity. There are eighteenth-century objects associated with Captain Cook from Hawaii and Tahiti in the Hunterian Museum and Art Gallery and the National Museums of Scotland. Other important Pacific material is in Paisley, Perth, the Marischal Museum, Aberdeen and Glasgow Museums. Stromness Museum has a few Pacific items which may also be associated with Captain Cook but further research is needed to verify this.

Material from the Americas, although the smallest proportion of objects in Scottish collections, includes rare items, such as a Salish cloak from the Northwest Coast of North America in Perth, and collections of eighteenth-century Native American material in the Marischal Museum, the National Museums of Scotland and the Hunterian Museum and Art Gallery in Glasgow. There are also groups of Pre-Columbian pottery and sculpture in Kirkcaldy Museum and Art Gallery, Nairn Literary Institute Museum, the National Museums of Scotland and Glasgow Museums.

Place-name Guides

Place-name Guide 1

Alphabetical listing	Heading in Summary Catalogue	Alphabetical listing	Heading in Summary Catalogue
Admiralty Islands	Melanesia	Fiji	Polynesia
Afghanistan	Central Asia		
Algeria	North Africa	Gabon	Central Africa
Amazonia	South America	Ghana	West Africa
Andean	South America	Great Basin	North America
Angola	Southern Africa	Guinea	West Africa
Arctic	North America	Guyana	South America
Argentina	South America		
Austral Islands	Polynesia	Hawaii	Polynesia
Australia	Australia	Honduras	Central America
Bahrain	Middle East	India	South Asia
Bali	South East Asia	India- Nagas	South Asia
Bangladesh	South Asia	Iran	Middle East
Bhutan	Central Asia	Irian Jaya	South East Asia
Benin Republic	West Africa	Israel	Middle East
Bismarck Archipelago	Melanesia	Ivory Coast	West Africa
Bolivia	South America		
Borneo	South East Asia	Japan	East Asia
Botswana	Southern Africa	Japan – Ainu	East Asia
Brazil	South America	Japan – Okinawa	East Asia
Brunei	South East Asia	Java	South East Asia
Burkina Faso	West Africa		
Burma	South East Asia	Kampuchea	South East Asia
		Kazakhstan	Central Asia
California	North America	Kenya	East Africa
Cameroun	Central Africa	Kirghizia	Central Asia
Canary Islands	North Africa	Kiribati	Micronesia
Caribbean	Central America	Korea	East Asia
Caroline Islands	Micronesia	Kuwait	Middle East
Central India	South Asia		
Chile	South America	Laos	South East Asia
China	East Asia	Liberia	West Africa
Colombia	South America	Libya	North Africa
Congo	Central Africa		
Costa Rica	Central America	Madagascar	Southern Africa
		Malawi	East Africa
		Malaysia	South East Asia
		Mali	West Africa
Easter Island	Polynesia	Mariana Islands	Micronesia
Ecuador	South America	Marquesas Islands	Polynesia
Egypt	North Africa	Mexico	Central America
Ethiopia	East Africa		

Alphabetical listing	Heading in Summary Catalogue	Alphabetical listing	Heading in Summary Catalogue
Maluku Islands	South East Asia	Sierra Leone	West Africa
Mongolia	East Asia	Society Islands	Polynesia
Morocco	North Africa	Solomon Islands	Melanesia
Mozambique	Southern Africa	Somalia	East Africa
		South Africa	Southern Africa
Namibia	Southern Africa	South India	South Asia
Nepal	Central Asia	South Korea	East Asia
New Britain	Melanesia	Southeast	North America
New Caledonia	Melanesia	Southwest	North America
New Ireland	Melanesia	Sri Lanka	South Asia
New Hebrides	Melanesia	Subarctic	North America
New Zealand	Polynesia	Sudan	North Africa
Nicaragua	Central America	Sulawesi	South East Asia
Nigeria	West Africa	Sumatra	South East Asia
Niue	Polynesia	Syria	Middle East
North India	South Asia		
North Korea	East Asia	Taiwan	East Asia
Northeast	North America	Tajikistan	Central Asia
Northwest Coast	North America	Tanzania	East Africa
North West Frontier Province	South Asia	Thailand	South East Asia
		Tibet	Central Asia
		Tokelau Islands	Polynesia
Oman	Middle East	Tonga	Polynesia
		Tunisia	North Africa
Pakistan	South Asia	Turkestan	Central Asia
Palestine	Middle East	Turkey	Middle East
Panama	Central America	Tuvalu	Micronesia
Papua New Guinea	Melanesia		
Paraguay	South America	Uganda	East Africa
Peru	South America	United Arab Emirates	Middle East
Philippines	South East Asia	Uruguay	South America
Plains	North America	Uzbekistan	Central Asia
Plateau	North America		
Pre-Columbian	Central America	Vanuatu	Melanesia
Pre-Columbian	South America	Venezuela	South America
		Vietnam	South East Asia
Qatar	Middle East		
		Yemen	Middle East
Rwanda-Burundi	Central Africa		
		Zaire	Central Africa
Sabah	South East Asia	Zambia	Southern Africa
Samoa	Polynesia	Zimbabwe	Southern Africa
Santa Cruz	Melanesia		
Sarawak	South East Asia		
Saudi Arabia	Middle East		
Senegal	West Africa		

Place-name Guide 2

Africa
North Africa
- Algeria
- Canary Islands
- Egypt
- Libya
- Morocco
- Sudan
- Tunisia

West Africa
- Benin Republic
- Burkina Faso
- Ghana
- Guinea
- Ivory Coast
- Liberia
- Mali
- Mauritania
- Nigeria
- Senegal
- Sierra Leone

Central Africa
- Cameroun
- Congo
- Gabon
- Rwanda-Burundi
- Zaire

East Africa
- Ethiopia
- Kenya
- Malawi
- Somalia
- Tanzania
- Uganda

Southern Africa
- Angola
- Botswana
- Madagascar
- Mozambique
- Namibia
- South Africa
- Zambia
- Zimbabwe

Americas
North America
- Arctic
- California
- Great Basin
- Northeast
- Northwest Coast
- Plains
- Plateau
- Southeast
- Southwest
- Subarctic

Central America
- Caribbean
- Costa Rica
- Honduras
- Mexico
- Nicaragua
- Panama
- Pre-Columbian

South America
- Amazonia
- Andean
- Argentina
- Bolivia
- Brazil
- Chile
- Colombia
- Ecuador
- Guyana
- Paraguay
- Peru
- Pre-Columbian
- Uruguay
- Venezuela

Asia
South East Asia
- Bali
- Borneo
- Brunei
- Burma
- Irian Jaya
- Java
- Kampuchea
- Laos
- Malaysia
- Maluku Islands
- Philippines
- Sabah
- Sarawak
- Sulawesi
- Sumatra
- Thailand
- Vietnam

Middle East
- Bahrain
- Egypt
- Iran
- Iraq
- Israel
- Kuwait
- Oman
- Palestine
- Qatar
- Saudi Arabia
- Syria
- Turkey
- United Arab Emirates
- Yemen

Central Asia
- Afghanistan
- Bhutan
- Kazakhstan
- Kirghizia
- Nepal
- Tajikistan
- Tibet
- Turkestan
- Uzbekistan

East Asia
- Ainu
- Inner Mongolia
- Japan
- Mongolia
- North Korea
- Okinawa
- Peoples Republic of China
- Sinkiang
- South Korea
- Xinjiang

South Asia
- Bangladesh
- Central India
- Indian Cultural Area
- Nagas
- North India
- NW Frontier Province
- Pakistan
- South India
- Sri Lanka

Oceania
Australia

Melanesia
- Admiralty Islands
- Bismarck Archipelago
- New Caledonia
- New Britain
- New Hebrides
- New Ireland
- Papua New Guinea
- Solomon Islands
- Santa Cruz
- Vanuatu

Polynesia
- Austral Islands
- Cook Islands
- Easter Island
- Fiji
- Hawaii
- Marquesas Islands
- New Zealand
- Niue
- Samoa
- Society Islands
- Tokelau Islands
- Tonga

Micronesia
- Caroline Islands
- Kiribati
- Mariana Islands
- Tuvalu

The Summary Catalogue

AFRICA

Abbotsford, Melrose (7)
Aberdeen Art Gallery and Museums (10)
Angus District Museums (29)
Dumfries Museum (63)
Dundee Art Galleries and Museums (138)
Dunrobin Castle Museum, Golspie (77)
Edinburgh University Collection of Historic Musical Instruments (171)
Elgin Museum (171)
Falconer Museum, Forres (26)
Hawick Museum (10)
Kirkcaldy Museum and Art Gallery (4)
Marischal Museum, Aberdeen (24)
McLean Museum and Art Gallery, Greenock (180)
Monklands District Council Museums, Coatbridge (21)
Museum of Childhood, Edinburgh (1)
Nairn Literary Institute Museum (1)
North East Fife District Museum Service (34)
Paisley Museum and Art Galleries (214)
Perth Museum and Art Gallery (58)
Smith Art Gallery and Museum, Stirling (38)
Strathaven, John Hastie Museum (1)
Stromness Museum, Orkney (12)
The Dick Institute, Kilmarnock (175)
The Cameronians (Scottish Rifles) Regimental Museum, Hamilton (12)
The Argyll and Sutherland Highlanders Regimental Museum, Stirling (1)
The David Livingstone Centre, Blantyre (188)
Tweeddale Museum, Peebles (10)
University of St Andrews (10)

NORTH AFRICA

Abbotsford, Melrose (1)
Angus District Museums (16)
Dumfries Museum (8)
Dundee Art Galleries and Museums (27)
Dunrobin Castle Museum, Golspie (9)
Edinburgh University Collection of Historic Musical Instruments (9)
Elgin Museum (100)
Falconer Museum, Forres (4)
Glasgow Museums, Kelvingrove (300) [see note 1]
Hawick Museum (8)
Hunterian Museum and Art Gallery, Glasgow (10)
Marischal Museum, Aberdeen (63)
McLean Museum and Art Gallery, Greenock (5)
Monklands District Council Museums, Coatbridge (2)

Museum of Childhood, Edinburgh (1)
Nairn Literary Institute Museum (16)
National Museums of Scotland (1048) [see note 1]
North Berwick Museum (1)
Paisley Museum and Art Galleries (19)
Perth Museum and Art Gallery (31)
Smith Art Gallery and Museum, Stirling (70)
The Black Watch Museum, Perth (12)
The Dick Institute, Kilmarnock (16)
Tweeddale Museum, Peebles (6)
University of St Andrews (4)

WEST AFRICA

Aberdeen Art Gallery and Museums (10)
Angus District Museums (64)
Dumfries Museum (6)
Dundee Art Galleries and Museums (587)
Dunrobin Castle Museum, Golspie (25)
Edinburgh University Collection of Historic Musical Instruments (10)
Elgin Museum (35)
Glasgow Museums, Kelvingrove (2000) [see note 1]
Hawick Museum (2)
Hunterian Museum and Art Gallery, Glasgow (398)
Inverness Museum and Art Gallery (1)
Kirkcaldy Museum and Art Gallery (19)
Marischal Museum, Aberdeen (1139)
McLean Museum and Art Gallery, Greenock (8)
Monklands District Council Museums, Coatbridge (11)
Museum of Childhood, Edinburgh (1)
Nairn Literary Institute Museum (74)
National Museums of Scotland (2600) [see note 1]
Paisley Museum and Art Galleries (96)
Perth Museum and Art Gallery (97)
Smith Art Gallery and Museum, Stirling (57)
Strathaven, John Hastie Museum (1)
Stromness Museum, Orkney (48)
Tain Museum (5)
The Dick Institute, Kilmarnock (48)
The Black Watch Museum, Perth (22)
The David Livingstone Centre, Blantyre (14)
Tweeddale Museum, Peebles (2)
University of St Andrews (10)

CENTRAL AFRICA

Aberdeen Art Gallery and Museums (1)
Angus District Museums (27)
Dundee Art Galleries and Museums (125)
Dunrobin Castle Museum, Golspie (28)

Edinburgh University Collection of Historic Musical Instruments (2)
Elgin Museum (31)
Falconer Museum, Forres (12)
Glasgow Museums, Kelvingrove (700) [see note 1]
Hawick Museum (2)
Hunterian Museum and Art Gallery, Glasgow (45)
Marischal Museum, Aberdeen (155)
McLean Museum and Art Gallery, Greenock (1)
Monklands District Council Museums, Coatbridge (2)
Museum of Childhood, Edinburgh (1)
National Museums of Scotland (1200) [see note 1]
North East Fife District Museum Service (2)
Paisley Museum and Art Galleries (7)
Perth Museum and Art Gallery (25)
Smith Art Gallery and Museum, Stirling (51)
Stromness Museum, Orkney (4)
The David Livingstone Centre, Blantyre (5)
The Dick Institute, Kilmarnock (24)
Tweeddale Museum, Peebles (3)

EAST AFRICA
Abbotsford, Melrose (1)
Angus District Museums (27)
Dumfries Museum (8)
Dundee Art Galleries and Museums (255)
Dunrobin Castle Museum, Golspie (49)
Edinburgh University Collection of Historic Musical Instruments (33)
Elgin Museum (41)
Glasgow Museums, Kelvingrove (500) [see note 1]
Hawick Museum (1)
Hunterian Museum and Art Gallery, Glasgow (200)
Kelburne Castle Museum, Fairlie (2)
Kirkcaldy Museum and Art Gallery (2)
Marischal Museum, Aberdeen (580)
McLean Museum and Art Gallery, Greenock (23)
Monklands District Council Museums, Coatbridge (14)
Museum of Childhood, Edinburgh (6)
Nairn Literary Institute Museum (11)
National Museums of Scotland (1600) [see note 1]
North East Fife District Museum Service (45)
Paisley Museum and Art Galleries (110)
Perth Museum and Art Gallery (70)
Smith Art Gallery and Museum, Stirling (38)
Stromness Museum, Orkney (1)
The Black Watch Museum, Perth (1)
The David Livingstone Centre, Blantyre (44)
The Cameronians (Scottish Rifles) Regimental Museum, Hamilton (15)
The Dick Institute, Kilmarnock (9)
Tweeddale Museum, Peebles (3)
University of St Andrews (4)
Wick Heritage Centre (1)

SOUTHERN AFRICA
Abbotsford, Melrose (3)
Aberdeen Art Gallery and Museums (12)
Angus District Museums (66)

Dumfries Museum (12)
Dundee Art Galleries and Museums (153)
Dunrobin Castle Museum, Golspie (105)
Edinburgh University Collection of Historic Musical Instruments (1)
Elgin Museum (33)
Falconer Museum, Forres (4)
Fochabers Folk Museum (5)
Glasgow Museums, Kelvingrove (500) [see note 1]
Hawick Museum (1)
Hunterian Museum and Art Gallery, Glasgow (251)
Inverness Museum and Art Gallery (1)
Kirkcaldy Museum and Art Gallery (4)
Lhaidhay Croft Museum, Dunbeath (1)
Marischal Museum, Aberdeen (417)
McLean Museum and Art Gallery, Greenock (26)
Monklands District Council Museums, Coatbridge (30)
Museum of Childhood, Edinburgh (9)
Nairn Literary Institute Museum (22)
National Museums of Scotland (300) [see note 1]
North East Fife District Museum Service (101)
Paisley Museum and Art Galleries (125)
Perth Museum and Art Gallery (141)
Smith Art Gallery and Museum, Stirling (410)
Stromness Museum, Orkney (10)
The Royal Scots Regimental Museum, Edinburgh (2)
The Dick Institute, Kilmarnock (54)
The Argyll and Sutherland Highlanders Regimental Museum, Stirling (5)
The David Livingstone Centre, Blantyre (70)
The National Trust for Scotland (3) [see note 2]
Wigtown Museum (3)

AMERICAS
Dumfries Museum (9)
Elgin Museum (1)
Marischal Museum, Aberdeen (4)
McLean Museum and Art Gallery, Greenock (5)
Nairn Literary Institute Museum (1)
Strathkelvin District Museums, Kirkintilloch (2)
Stromness Museum, Orkney (2)
The Stewartry Museum, Kirkcudbright (7)

NORTH AMERICA
Abbotsford, Melrose (6)
Aberdeen Art Gallery and Museums (12)
Angus District Museums (43)
Dumfries Museum (3)
Dundee Art Galleries and Museums (214)
Dunrobin Castle Museum, Golspie (14)
Edinburgh City Arts Centre (1)
Elgin Museum (40)
Falconer Museum, Forres (7)
Glasgow Museums, Kelvingrove (480) [see note 1]
Hawick Museum (1)
Hunterian Museum and Art Gallery, Glasgow (210)
Marischal Museum, Aberdeen (1134)
McLean Museum and Art Gallery, Greenock (9)
Museum of Childhood, Edinburgh (1)

Nairn Literary Institute Museum (15)
National Museums of Scotland (1600) [see note 1]
North East Fife District Museum Service (2)
North East of Scotland Museums Service (1)
Paisley Museum and Art Galleries (35)
Perth Museum and Art Gallery (403)
Shetland Museum (7)
Smith Art Gallery and Museum, Stirling (258)
Strathaven, John Hastie Museum (5)
Strathkelvin District Museums, Kirkintilloch (1)
Stromness Museum, Orkney (32)
Tain Museum (2)
The Stewartry Museum, Kirkcudbright (37)
The Royal Scots Regimental Museum, Edinburgh (3)
The National Trust for Scotland (3)
The Dick Institute, Kilmarnock (6)
The Argyll and Sutherland Highlanders Regimental
Museum, Stirling (1)
The David Livingstone Centre, Blantyre (2)
University of St Andrews (4)
Wigtown Museum (3)

CENTRAL AMERICA
Abbotsford, Melrose (14)
Angus District Museums (3)
Dumfries Museum (6)
Dundee Art Galleries and Museums (12)
Elgin Museum (122)
Glasgow Museums, Kelvingrove (120) [see note 1]
Hunterian Museum and Art Gallery, Glasgow (68)
Kirkcaldy Museum and Art Gallery (4)
Marischal Museum, Aberdeen (1152)
McLean Museum and Art Gallery, Greenock (12)
Museum of Childhood, Edinburgh (12)
National Museums of Scotland (700) [see note 1]
North East of Scotland Museums Service (1)
Paisley Museum and Art Galleries (13)
Perth Museum and Art Gallery (24)
Smith Art Gallery and Museum, Stirling (78)
Strathkelvin District Museums, Kirkintilloch (5)
Stromness Museum, Orkney (5)
The Dick Institute, Kilmarnock (4)

SOUTH AMERICA
Andrew Carnegie Birthplace Museum, Dunfermline (1)
Angus District Museums (32)
Dumfries Museum (4)
Dundee Art Galleries and Museums (9)
Edinburgh University Collection of Historic Musical
Instruments (1)
Elgin Museum (28)
Glasgow Museums, Kelvingrove (1200) [see note 1]
Hawick Museum (5)
Hunterian Museum and Art Gallery, Glasgow (123)
Kirkcaldy Museum and Art Gallery (50)
Marischal Museum, Aberdeen (369)
McLean Museum and Art Gallery, Greenock (33)
Nairn Literary Institute Museum (24)
National Museums of Scotland (2000) [see note 1]

North East Fife District Museum Service (5)
Paisley Museum and Art Galleries (36)
Perth Museum and Art Gallery (41)
Smith Art Gallery and Museum, Stirling (56)
Stromness Museum, Orkney (19)
The Dick Institute, Kilmarnock (11)
Tweeddale Museum, Peebles (10)
University of St Andrews (112)

ASIA
Aberdeen Art Gallery and Museums (1)
Angus District Museums (1)
Dumfries Museum (22)
Dundee Art Galleries and Museums (38)
Dunrobin Castle Museum, Golspie (17)
Elgin Museum (2)
Hawick Museum (9)
Hunterian Museum and Art Gallery, Glasgow (3)
Inverness Museum and Art Gallery (2)
Kirkcaldy Museum and Art Gallery (11)
McLean Museum and Art Gallery, Greenock (2)
Monklands District Council Museums, Coatbridge (3)
North East Fife District Museum Service (13)
North East of Scotland Museums Service (1)
North Berwick Museum (4)
Paisley Museum and Art Galleries (97)
Perth Museum and Art Gallery (2)
Smith Art Gallery and Museum, Stirling (36)
Strathaven, John Hastie Museum (2)
Stromness Museum, Orkney (3)
The Dick Institute, Kilmarnock (29)
Tweeddale Museum, Peebles (1)
University of St Andrews (4)

SOUTH EAST ASIA
Abbotsford, Melrose (12)
Aberdeen Art Gallery and Museums (2)
Angus District Museums (27)
Dumfries Museum (4)
Dundee Art Galleries and Museums (91)
Dunrobin Castle Museum, Golspie (3)
Edinburgh University Collection of Historic Musical
Instruments (7)
Elgin Museum (56)
Ettrick and Lauderdale District Museums Service,
Selkirk (1)
Falconer Museum, Forres (16)
Glasgow Museums, Kelvingrove (800) Burrell (no number) [see note 1]
Hawick Museum (7)
Hunterian Museum and Art Gallery, Glasgow (275)
Kelburne Castle Museum, Fairlie (3)
Kirkcaldy Museum and Art Gallery (26)
Marischal Museum, Aberdeen (275)
McLean Museum and Art Gallery, Greenock (43)
Monklands District Council Museums, Coatbridge (2)
Museum of Childhood, Edinburgh (7)
Nairn Literary Institute Museum (9)
National Museums of Scotland (2277) [see note 1]

North East Fife District Museum Service (11)
Paisley Museum and Art Galleries (19)
Perth Museum and Art Gallery (354)
Smith Art Gallery and Museum, Stirling (113)
Strathaven, John Hastie Museum (1)
Stromness Museum, Orkney (2)
The Black Watch Museum, Perth (10)
The Argyll and Sutherland Highlanders Regimental Museum, Stirling (13)
The Cameronians (Scottish Rifles) Regimental Museum, Hamilton (3)
The Dick Institute, Kilmarnock (46)
The National Trust for Scotland (2) [see note 2]
The Royal Scots Regimental Museum, Edinburgh (1)
Tweeddale Museum, Peebles (4)
University of St Andrews (7)

MIDDLE EAST
Abbotsford, Melrose (17)
Angus District Museums (11)
Dundee Art Galleries and Museums (8)
Edinburgh University Collection of Historic Musical Instruments (1)
Elgin Museum (23)
Falconer Museum, Forres (2)
Glasgow Museums, Kelvingrove (500), Burrell Collection (450) [see note 1]
Hawick Museum (5)
Hunterian Museum and Art Gallery, Glasgow (51)
Inverness Museum and Art Gallery (1)
Kelburne Castle, Fairlie (7)
Kirkcaldy Museum and Art Gallery (3)
Marischal Museum, Aberdeen (3)
McLean Museum and Art Gallery, Greenock (7)
Monklands District Council Museums, Coatbridge (1)
Museum of Childhood, Edinburgh (2)
National Museums of Scotland (447) [see note 1]
Perth Museum and Art Gallery (24)
Smith Art Gallery and Museum, Stirling (4)
Strathkelvin District Museums, Kirkintilloch (1)
The Dick Institute, Kilmarnock (5)
The Black Watch Museum, Perth (8)
Tweeddale Museum, Peebles (3)

CENTRAL ASIA
Abbotsford, Melrose (1)
Angus District Museums (4)
Dumfries Museum (18)
Dundee Art Galleries and Museums (52)
Edinburgh University Collection of Historic Musical Instruments (4)
Elgin Museum (7)
Glasgow Museums, Burrell Collection (11) [see note 1]
Hawick Museum (1)
Hunterian Museum and Art Gallery, Glasgow (17)
Kelburne Castle Museum, Fairlie (2)
Marischal Museum, Aberdeen (8)
McLean Museum and Art Gallery, Greenock (3)
National Museums of Scotland (2376) [see note 1]

Paisley Museum and Art Galleries (5)
Perth Museum and Art Gallery (44)
Smith Art Gallery and Museum, Stirling (16)
The Dick Institute, Kilmarnock (7)
Tweeddale Museum, Peebles (2)
University of St Andrews (3)

EAST ASIA
Abbotsford, Melrose (11)
Aberdeen Art Gallery and Museums (159)
Andrew Carnegie Birthplace Museum, Dunfermline (4)
Angus District Museums (135)
Dumfries Museum (129)
Dundee Art Galleries and Museums (158)
Dunrobin Castle Museum, Golspie (4)
Edinburgh University Collection of Historic Musical Instruments (32)
Elgin Museum (224)
Falconer Museum, Forres (72)
Glasgow Museums, Kelvingrove (3000), Burrell Collection (1712) [see note 1]
Hawick Museum (36)
Hunterian Museum and Art Gallery, Glasgow (85)
Inverness Museum and Art Gallery (20)
Kelburne Castle, Fairlie (19)
Kirkcaldy Museum and Art Gallery (142)
Marischal Museum, Aberdeen (37)
McLean Museum and Art Gallery, Greenock (456)
Monklands District Council Museums, Coatbridge (1)
Museum of Childhood, Edinburgh (23)
Nairn Literary Institute Museum (38)
National Museums of Scotland (17463) [see note 1]
North East Fife District Museum Service (6)
North East of Scotland Museums Service (49)
Paisley Museum and Art Galleries (135)
Perth Museum and Art Gallery (616)
Shetland Museum (2)
Smith Art Gallery and Museum, Stirling (866)
Stromness Museum, Orkney (20)
The Dick Institute, Kilmarnock (60)
The Black Watch Museum, Perth (7)
The Argyll and Sutherland Highlanders Regimental Museum, Stirling (2)
The Cameronians (Scottish Rifles) Regimental Museum, Hamilton (3)
The Royal Scots Regimental Museum, Edinburgh (4)
Tweeddale Museum, Peebles (12)
University of St Andrews (1)

SOUTH ASIA
Abbotsford, Melrose (29)
Angus District Museums (10)
Dumfries Museum (38)
Dundee Art Galleries and Museums (211)
Dunrobin Castle Museum, Golspie (171)
Edinburgh University Collection of Historic Musical Instruments (12)
Elgin Museum (245)

Ettrick and Lauderdale District Museums Service, Selkirk (1)

Falconer Museum, Forres (129)

Glasgow Museums, Kelvingrove (2700), Burrell (13) [see note 1]

Hawick Museum (40)

Hunterian Museum and Art Gallery, Glasgow (212)

Inverness Museum and Art Gallery (15)

Kelburne Castle Museum, Fairlie (11)

Kirkcaldy Museum and Art Gallery (30)

Marischal Museum, Aberdeen (326)

McLean Museum and Art Gallery, Greenock (67)

Museum of Childhood, Edinburgh (38)

Nairn Literary Institute Museum (39)

National Museums of Scotland (1734) [see note 1]

North East Fife District Museum Service (31)

North Berwick Museum (6)

Paisley Museum and Art Galleries (112)

Perth Museum and Art Gallery (522)

Smith Art Gallery and Museum, Stirling (321)

Strathaven, John Hastie Museum (5)

Stromness Museum, Orkney (15)

Tain Museum (1)

The Stewartry Museum, Kirkcudbright (1)

The Black Watch Museum, Perth (17)

The David Livingstone Centre, Blantyre (4)

The Dick Institute, Kilmarnock (134)

The Argyll and Sutherland Highlanders Regimental Museum, Stirling (10)

The National Trust for Scotland (1) [see note 2]

The Royal Scots Regimental Museum, Edinburgh (5)

The Rozelle Galleries, Alloway (5)

The Cameronians (Scottish Rifles) Regimental Museum, Hamilton (1)

Tweeddale Museum, Peebles (65)

University of St Andrews (6)

OCEANIA

Abbotsford, Melrose (9)

Angus District Museums (10)

Dumfries Museum (6)

Dundee Art Galleries and Museums (28)

Edinburgh University Collection of Historic Musical Instruments (3)

Elgin Museum (10)

Hawick Museum (1)

Kelburne Castle Museum, Fairlie (2)

Marischal Museum, Aberdeen (5)

McLean Museum, Greenock (4)

Monklands District Council Museums, Coatbridge (3)

Nairn Literary Institute Museum (2)

North Berwick Museum (2)

North East Fife District Museum Service (15)

Paisley Museum and Art Galleries (116)

Smith Art Gallery and Museum, Stirling (3)

The Rozelle Galleries, Alloway (4)

The Dick Institute, Kilmarnock (56)

The Stewartry Museum, Kirkcudbright (1)

University of St Andrews (1)

AUSTRALIA

Angus District Museums (39)

Dumfries Museum (13)

Dundee Art Galleries and Museums (23)

Dunrobin Castle Museum, Golspie (1)

Edinburgh University Collection of Historic Musical Instruments (2)

Elgin Museum (5)

Falconer Museum, Forres (11)

Glasgow Museums, Kelvingrove (350) [see note 1]

Hawick Museum (2)

Hunterian Museum and Art Gallery, Glasgow (224)

Kirkcaldy Museum and Art Gallery (11)

Marischal Museum, Aberdeen (316)

McLean Museum and Art Gallery, Greenock (25)

Monklands District Council Museums, Coatbridge (2)

Nairn Literary Institute Museum (15)

National Museums of Scotland (800) [see note 1]

North Berwick Museum (1)

North East of Scotland Museums Service (1)

North East Fife District Museum Service (17)

Paisley Museum and Art Galleries (87)

Perth Museum and Art Gallery (81)

Smith Art Gallery and Museum, Stirling (19)

The Argyll and Sutherland Highlanders Regimental Museum, Stirling (1)

The Dick Institute, Kilmarnock (39)

The Rozelle Galleries, Alloway (1)

The Stewartry Museum, Kirkcudbright (7)

Tweeddale Museum, Peebles (1)

University of St Andrews (5)

Wick Heritage Centre (1)

MELANESIA

Aberdeen Art Gallery and Museums (1)

Angus District Museums (91)

Dumfries Museum (4)

Dundee Art Galleries and Museums (93)

Dunrobin Castle Museum, Golspie (16)

Elgin Museum (20)

Falconer Museum, Forres (66)

Glasgow Museums, Kelvingrove (980) [see note 1]

Hawick Museum (8)

Hunterian Museum and Art Gallery, Glasgow (240)

Inverness Museum and Art Gallery (1)

John Hastie Museum, Strathaven (1)

Kirkcaldy Museum and Art Gallery (13)

Marischal Museum, Aberdeen (818)

McLean Museum and Art Gallery, Greenock (139)

Monklands District Council Museums, Coatbridge (9)

Nairn Literary Institute Museum (20)

National Museums of Scotland (1500) [see note 1]

North East Fife District Museum Service (80)

Paisley Museum and Art Galleries (24)

Perth Museum and Art Gallery (244)

Smith Art Gallery and Museum, Stirling (277)

Stromness Museum, Orkney (1)

The David Livingstone Centre, Blantyre (1)

The Dick Institute, Kilmarnock (66)

The National Trust for Scotland (3) [see note 2]
The Rozelle Galleries, Alloway (5)
The Stewartry Museum, Kirkcudbright (1)
University of St Andrews (2)

POLYNESIA

Abbotsford, Melrose (4)
Andrew Carnegie Birthplace Museum, Dunfermline (1)
Angus District Museums (65)
Dumfries Museum (2)
Dundee Art Galleries and Museums (60)
Dunrobin Castle Museum, Golspie (1)
Edinburgh University Collection of Historic Musical
    Instruments (1)
Elgin Museum (20)
Ettrick and Lauderdale District Museums Service,
    Selkirk (1)
Falconer Museum, Forres (17)
Glasgow Museums, Kelvingrove (350) [see note 1]
Hawick Museum (3)
Hunterian Museum and Art Gallery, Glasgow (394)
Inverness Museum and Art Gallery (3)
Kelburne Castle Museum, Fairlie (6)
Kirkcaldy Museum and Art Gallery (3)
Marischal Museum, Aberdeen (185)
McLean Museum and Art Gallery, Greenock (15)
Monklands District Council Museums, Coatbridge (6)
Nairn Literary Institute Museum (5)
National Museums of Scotland (1200) [see note 1]
North East Fife District Museum Service (29)
Paisley Museum and Art Galleries (28)
Perth Museum and Art Gallery (190)
Smith Art Gallery and Museum, Stirling (27)
Stromness Museum, Orkney (12)
The Cameronians (Scottish Rifles) Regimental Museum,
    Hamilton (1)
The Dick Institute, Kilmarnock (1)
The National Trust for Scotland (1) [Isee note 2]
The Rozelle Galleries, Alloway (12)
The Stewartry Museum, Kirkcudbright (8)
Tweeddale Museum, Peebles (1)
University of St Andrews (5)
Wigtown Museum (1)

MICRONESIA

Angus District Museums (14)
Dumfries Museum (1)
Dundee Art Galleries and Museums (6)
Dunrobin Castle Museum, Golspie (1)
Falconer Museum, Forres (1)
Glasgow Museums, Kelvingrove (20) [see note 1]
Hunterian Museum and Art Gallery, Glasgow (10)
Marischal Museum, Aberdeen (21)
McLean Museum and Art Gallery, Greenock (1)
National Museums of Scotland (180) [see note 1]
Paisley Museum and Art Galleries (1)
Perth Museum and Art Gallery (4)
Smith Art Gallery and Museum, Stirling (7)
Stromness Museum, Orkney (1)

UNPROVENANCED (see note 3)

Abbotsford, Melrose (31)
Aberdeen Art Gallery and Museums (1)
Andrew Carnegie Birthplace Museum, Dunfermline (8)
Angus District Museums (81)
Dumfries Museum (73)
Dundee Art Galleries and Museums (386)
Dunrobin Castle Museum, Golspie (176)
Edinburgh University Collection of Historic Musical
Instruments (9)
Elgin Museum (18)
Falconer Museum, Forres (195)
Fochabers Folk Museum (1)
Hawick Museum (32)
Hunterian Museum and Art Gallery, Glasgow (110)
Inverness Museum and Art Gallery (27)
Kelburne Castle Museum, Fairlie (4)
Kirkcaldy Museum and Art Gallery (10)
Marischal Museum, Aberdeen (2503) [see note 3]
McLean Museum and Art Gallery, Greenock (200)
Monklands District Council Museums, Coatbridge (53)
Museum of Childhood, Edinburgh (28)
Nairn Literary Institute Museum (16)
North Berwick Museum (1)
North East of Scotland Museums Service (687)
Paisley Museum and Art Galleries (259)
Perth Museum and Art Gallery (152)
Shetland Museum (12)
Smith Art Gallery and Museum, Stirling (61)
Strathkelvin District Museums, Kirkintilloch (10)
Stromness Museum, Orkney (61)
The Argyll and Sutherland Highlanders Regimental
Museum, Stirling (2)
The Cameronians (Scottish Rifles) Regimental
    Museum (4)
The David Livingstone Centre, Blantyre (398)
The Dick Institute, Kilmarnock (185)
The National Trust for Scotland (2) [see note 2]
The Royal Scots Regimental Museum, Edinburgh (3)
The Rozelle Galleries, Alloway (4)
The Stewartry Museum, Kirkcudbright (1)
Tweeddale Museum, Peebles (31)
University of St Andrews (23)
Wick Heritage Centre (1)
Wigtown Museum (1)

Notes

1 At the time of writing the records of the two largest collections, those of the National Museums of Scotland and Glasgow Museums, are not yet fully computerised. Approximately 85% of the foreign ethnography collection records of the National Museums of Scotland is retrievable through the National Database. Work is presently underway to computerise documentation throughout Glasgow Museums. Figures for Glasgow Museums holdings are based on collection summaries provided by the Curator.

2 The National Trust is currently revising the inventory of items in its care.

3 This figure for unprovenanced material is misleading. A significant contributing factor is that there is a number of groups of material for which each item has an accession record and has therefore been entered as a discrete record on the National Database. Details of provenance, donor, date, etc, appear only in the first record of an accession series and are omitted from other records in the group at this stage. It is envisaged that this will be rectified on the National Database in due course.

PART III: THE MANAGEMENT AND USE OF COLLECTIONS OF FOREIGN ETHNOGRAPHY

Presenting Other Cultures

Barbara Woroncow

Ethnographic collections in museums have been subject to varying fortunes in the past two hundred years. Eighteenth-century voyages of exploration aroused tremendous interest in exotic artefacts from overseas and items collected were successfully exhibited to the public as private, commercial ventures as well as being displayed in learned society and other museums.

On a national level, popular interest in the lives and crafts of people in other countries was generated by the great exhibitions from the mid-nineteenth century onwards. In terms of museum display, eighteenth-century collections of curios gave way to more didactic exhibitions. Large numbers of objects, often grouped by broad geographical areas, were shown with relatively brief labels. Some museums organised their displays on a cross-cultural basis, with sections covering topics such as fire-making or beadwork. Although there was significant interest in objects and their technology, little attempt was made to put them into the context of the societies from which they came.

In the middle of the twentieth century, the discipline of social anthropology moved away from the study of material culture towards areas such as kinship and economics, and therefore there was little progress in developing new approaches to display. In the post-war period, the display of many surviving collections either remained unchanged from the nineteenth-century style, or else reflected an uneven interest in "primitive art", mainly represented by figure sculpture and masks.

Since the late 1970s several factors have led to a renaissance of interest in collections of foreign ethnography: the recognition by social anthropologists that social institutions are manifested in and supported by material objects; the desire to promote multicultural understanding; an increased interest in arts and crafts techniques (eg. handloom weaving) and general concern for the conservation of our vanishing world heritage in terms both of the environment and the traditional forms of society within it. Public interest in other cultures and awareness of their problems has also been fuelled by increasing numbers of television documentaries and the recent growth in long-haul holidays.

Uses of Collections of Foreign Ethnography

At first sight, ethnographic collections may seem difficult to use within the context of a local museum. Field collecting is limited by the portability of objects and some nineteenth-century collections are overly weighted with weapons and basketry. Many items were brought back as single pieces by sailors, missionaries and other travellers. The majority of collections are trapped in a time warp between 1880 and 1920 and reflect societies which have now changed beyond all recognition, or have even vanished altogether. More contemporary collecting is urgently needed to balance older collections and demonstrate cultural change and continuity through the influence of trade goods, population movements and changing resources.

Recent display initiatives have increasingly sought the advice and active participation of local ethnic communities or members of the cultures or countries from which the collections originated. Both permanent galleries and temporary exhibitions have benefited from such liaisons in choosing display themes, drafting the text and securing additional loans. Close involvement and consultation is often a slow and time-consuming process, but one which brings immense rewards in terms of mutual understanding, cooperation and accuracy.

In dealing with the complexity of human societies and their material culture, no single approach to display can be considered as the "correct" one. There is scope to look at whole cultures, whether or not they are related to communities in this country. It can also be appropriate to isolate single objects and consider them in terms of their aesthetic qualities or craft skills. Alternatively, it may be desirable to look at some aspects of life on a cross-cultural basis to see how societies all over the world have coped with basic human needs such as food, shelter and beliefs. A diversity of approach is needed to deal with the diversity of human cultures.

Ethnographic collections are also valuable components of an area's local history, reflecting travel, trade and other contacts with far-flung places. Such collections form irreplaceable archives of material which can expand the current horizons of museum visitors of all ages and from all walks of life. The objects can arouse interest, excite admiration and develop insights into other ways of life, not only as part of the school curriculum, but also as the starting point for many other kinds of events and activities as the examples presented below indicate. Ethnographic collections may be employed in many different ways. They do not have to be used separately from the rest of the museum's collections and may be successfully integrated with local history or other disciplines.

Occasionally, particular care needs to be taken in order to avoid problems of an ethical nature. Great care is needed to ensure that religious or ceremonial items are displayed in such a way as to avoid giving unintentional offence. Language used in foreign ethnography records and labels needs to be chosen with care (McCorry, 1991). Further advice may need to be obtained from community representatives or specialist ethnographic curators (see Appendix 2). Curators of collections which include military trophies have a particular responsibility to consider issues such as the impact of imperialism with tact and sensitivity.

Collections of foreign ethnography may be used in a number of ways: to promote multicultural understanding; as an inspiration for art, craft and design studies; as a resource for considering "green issues" and to enhance local history. Posing questions may help: how do other societies cope with similar problems such as shelter and food?; how are events such as marriage or naming/christening ceremonies similar or different in other societies?; what are the origins and traditions of Scotland's communities?; how and why and when did these collections arrive here? was this due to the activities of local people overseas?

Collections of foreign ethnography also have wide use as sources for design, manufacturing techniques and skill development in many aspects of art and craft including the fields of textile decoration, drawing and print-making. Green issues such as rainforest conservation and environmental studies, resource issues such as land rights and drought, and world trade and its associated problems are areas of concern which may be clearly illustrated using foreign ethnographic collections.

Often, of course, these various contexts overlap one another. As a result, foreign ethnographic collections provide a rich resource for cross-curricular education projects such as Environmental Studies. They can also be used to support course work in English, Art, Technology and many other subjects.

The range of examples below illustrates ways in which museums of all types and sizes can use ethnographic collections for the benefit of their local communities, as well as for visitors from further afield. Such collections have a particular potential to excite interest and admiration from visitors whose contact with objects in everyday life is often limited to mass-produced goods which show little evidence of individual craftsmanship.

1: Anthropology Gallery, Marischal Museum, Marischal College, University of Aberdeen 'About Human Beings: About Being Human'
Charles Hunt

With the appointment of the University's first professional curator in 1979, the priority was to 'modernise' the museum's displays both physically and in content. Reopened in 1985 under the new name of the Marischal Museum, the gallery communicates modernity with mezzanine floors supported by exposed steel columns and weldmesh panels supporting objects and graphics. The display consists of objects from diverse eras and places grouped around themes such as the Human Family, Woman the Provider, Man the Hunter, Childhood, Seniority, Chiefs, Priests, the Natural World and so forth. Artefacts are not only from overseas cultures, but also from the immediate locality. For example, the 'Rites of Passage' section is illustrated with a photograph of University of Aberdeen graduation ceremonies as well as more exotic foreign artefacts. Such an approach can help in emphasising the recurrent common patterns within human societies rather than isolating differences between them.

Graphic illustrations, titles and bold generalisations about the human condition seek to identify the visitor with the objects and peoples on display. Captions and subsidiary graphics carry opinions and ideas drawn from anthropology as well as a broader literature, and work to support the more subjective, bold and thematic statements which may otherwise seem implausible. The gallery has used a mixed collection of ethnographic material and graphic devices to set the local population into a world context.

2: Glasgow Museums: St Mungo's Museum of Religious Life and Art
Antonia Lovelace

Glasgow Museums have had a separate gallery of ethnography since they opened in 1902. Now, for the first time, in the new St Mungo's Museum of Religious Life and Art, foreign ethnography is intermingled with ethnographic and historical material from Britain and Europe in a truly multicultural way.

St Mungo's has three permanent display galleries: an Art gallery, a gallery of comparative religions called the Religious Life gallery, and a Scottish gallery. In the Art gallery a newly acquired bronze statue of Shiva stands opposite paintings of Adam and Eve by William Blake. Near Dali's painting of St. John on the Cross are three Buddhist pieces, from Burma, Japan and China. Ranged opposite are an Egyptian mummy mask, a modern example of Islamic calligraphy and a seventeenth-century Turkish prayer rug from the Burrell collection. The Nigerian Kalabari ancestral screen is seen to much better effect in this more spacious layout than in its previous home in the African ethnography displays at Kelvingrove.

In the gallery of comparative religion, the life-cycle displays contrast mother and child images from Europe (the Virgin Mary and Jesus), Ancient Egypt (Isis and Horus), and China (Guanyin with a baby), in the case on Birth and Childhood. Coming of Age material for a Jewish boy's Bar Mitzvah is next to Kuba initiation masks from Zaire. After Marriage and Death a large display case focuses on ideas of the afterlife in different cultures. The six major world faiths, Buddhism, Christianity, Hinduism, Islam, Judaism, and Sikhism, each have a small display, in alphabetical order. Other topics covered include the overlap of politics and religion in Divine Rule, and the religious aspects of Persecution, War and Peace.

In the Scottish gallery there is a strong emphasis on the many faiths that have come to Scotland from pre-Christian times to the present day, with a synopsis of the history of the different communities that make up Glasgow today. One of the most important items is a cast-iron toilet sign reading "Lascars only" in English and Bengali, recently found in the Glasgow docks, which provides evidence of the treatment of Asian sailors in Glasgow around 1900.

There is a small temporary exhibition space in St. Mungo's. The Buddhist foundation of Samye Ling in the Scottish Borders provided an exhibition of thangkas painted in Scotland by their Tibetan master painter as the first exhibition to coincide with the opening of the new museum in April 1993.

A guidebook prepared for the museum has six pages at the end listing the numerous advisors and contributors who helped to bring the project to fruition. As expected, there have been complaints from some people about aspects of the representation of their faith and both curators and designers will remain open to discussion on the permanent display arrangements. This will be a continuing process.

3: Dundee Art Galleries and Museums : The Ethnography Collections
Janice Murray

Dundee Museums have ethnographic collections of over 2,500 items from Africa, Asia, North America and Oceania. The ethnographic collections are curated by the Human History Department. Without a specialist ethnography curator the museum is wary of attempting a full-blown ethnographic display, although in recent years parts of the collection have been successfully integrated into temporary exhibitions.

'The Miles Tae Dundee: the multicultural history of a city' looked at the growth of the city over the last 150 years with particular reference to its multicultural history. The exhibition took the view that, while there is no such thing as a common culture in the city, there is certainly a commonality of experience. This enabled the

use of the Asian Indian collection in the earliest parts of the exhibition while more contemporary experiences were illustrated by the reconstruction of a Sikh wedding scene.

A similar approach was used in the exhibition 'Hearts and Flowers - wedding customs and costume across the world'. As it was the first display in a new costume gallery a popular subject was chosen, but instead of going for acres of white tulle it was decided to approach the display through the cross-cultural themes associated with marriage such as special clothes, special food, dancing and celebration, fertility and contraception, religious rites and gift giving. Although the majority of the examples remained European if not Scottish, it was possible to include material such as a Sikh wedding sari, a Malayan bridegroom's outfit, and "Bunga telor", the eggs given by a Malayan bride's mother to wedding guests - similar in idea to Scottish favours and Italian Bomboniere. Photographic material enabled a widening of the scope to include Chinese and Jewish customs.

The museum is currently planning its next costume display and one idea is to develop the subject of silk. As well as showing the nineteenth-century 'posh frocks', examples of the Chinese and Japanese collections will be displayed.

4: Ethnographic Collections at the Laing Museum, Newburgh
Gillian Wilson

The Laing Museum is part of North East Fife District Museum Service. The ethnographic collection contains predominantly Oceanic objects and material from southern and central Africa. A small part of the Oceanic collection is on long-term display in the 'Victorian Scotland' gallery at the Laing Museum, Newburgh, where it is used to illustrate Scottish emigration to Australia and New Zealand in the mid-nineteenth century. The objects on display are all from Fiji and illustrate the use of two common raw materials, coconut fibre and the bark of the paper mulberry. They are displayed together with general statistics about emigration from Scotland, local emigration from Newburgh and information about the political and socio-economic connections between Fiji and New Zealand in the nineteenth century.

A large decorated barkcloth 'mosquito blanket' is probably the most striking item in the display. This barkcloth has provided the focus for 'barkcloth making' workshops for local children. The workshops begin in the display gallery where the museum's displays discuss different levels of technology, alternative ways of making cloth, look at the stages of making a large 'mosquito blanket' and the status attached to barkcloth in nineteenth-century Fiji. The children are then given stencils of the basic shapes used to decorate the barkcloth and first design their own barkcloth square and then paint it using similar colours to those on the original. The squares made in one session were glued together and are now used as a blind in one of the museum's windows.

5: Using the Ethnography Collection at the McLean Museum and Art Gallery, Greenock
Valerie Boa

As part of the Museum's development strategy it was decided to fully use the ethnographic collection in both long-term display and temporary exhibitions. The refurbished gallery currently displays examples of Asian and Oceanic material.

The contemporary relevance of the collection is in the following areas:
1. The ethnographic collection marks an important contribution to the social history of the area. It is a material record of the travels and activities of people from Inverclyde.
2. Ethnographic collections provide an important historical context for the increased awareness of the many cultural influences and beliefs that form part of contemporary society.
3. The collection is a valuable resource for educational activity.
4. An important theme in the Museum's displays is conservation. Displaying ethnographic material increases the visitor's awareness of the need to preserve the world's cultural heritage.

Since opening to the public in 1990 the displays have proved attractive to visitors. School parties of all ages regularly visit and the collection is readily accepted and enjoyed. Awareness of the collection amongst schools has resulted in requests for specific small displays of artefacts which they have used to supplement classwork in particular areas. The collection is used by children as an inspirational resource. For example, during a recent T-shirt painting activity, the art of New Ireland was used by a participant as a basis for a T-shirt pattern.

To supplement the longer-term displays the Museum has initiated a series of smaller temporary displays which concentrate on specific areas or issues. Currently a display to mark the UN Year of Indigenous Peoples is on show. This will be followed by 'Tsuba - The Art of the Japanese Swordguard'. Other small exhibitions are currently in preparation.

6: 'Discovering Japan': A temporary exhibition at the National Museums of Scotland
Barbara Woroncow

Ethnography does not only deal with people's lives in the past. It is also a means of looking at how other societies are responding to late twentieth-century pressures such as population growth, industrialisation and new technology.

As part of the UK-wide Japan Festival in 1991, the National Museums of Scotland presented a highly innovative, hands-on exhibition of contemporary and traditional Japanese culture. Designed to appeal to all visitors, the show reflected the past, present and future of Japan through eight themes such as costume, food and gardens. Visitors could try on a kimono, learn how to write a few words in Japanese, design a garden or a family crest, as well as glimpsing the future in the form of a reconstructed Space Hotel room. Cooking ingredients were seen and sniffed, and the intricate craft of present-wrapping could be attempted. Demonstrators were available to assist the public in trying out the various activities. Before leaving, visitors were invited to present a wish or have their fortune told at a Shinto shrine.

The exhibition was extremely popular and admissions were limited by timed tickets to 25 people at a time. In addition to the 'hands-on' element, the displays included interactive computer programmes, models and conventional labelling. The show's impact was further enhanced by an extensive programme of lectures and practical workshops on a variety of topics from contemporary design to kite-making. The exhibition was shown in Aberdeen Art Gallery and Museums and subsequently has been touring the UK under the auspices of the Japan Festival Education Trust.

The key themes of active participation and discovery learning were made possible by the extensive use of commercially available contemporary objects and materials which were not subject to the usually stringent controls on environmental standards and handling procedures. The use of contemporary material not only enabled the objects to be used and handled but, perhaps even more importantly, it clearly demonstrated the continuity of Japanese traditions into present-day life.

Further Information about the Use of Collections of Foreign Ethnography

Further information for curators seeking to extend the use of their ethnographic collections is available from the Library and Information Service of the Scottish Museums Council, the Museum Ethnographers Group and specialist ethnography curators.

Museum Abstracts (Scottish Museums Council, 1985-) may be used to track down examples of uses of foreign ethnographic collections which have been published nationally and internationally. *Evaluating Artefacts* (Centre for Multicultural Education, Leicester / Leicestershire Museums Arts and Records Service) addresses the use of museum objects as primary sources in the school curriculum.

It is hoped that the database resulting from the Foreign Ethnographic Collections Research Programme will enable such collections to be used in new and ever more imaginative ways in the future. It will provide greater opportunities for loans between museums to enhance exhibitions and other interpretive projects.

Although the lives of many societies have now been recorded on film and video, it is important to recognise that no media presentation can fully substitute for contact with "the real thing", although it can be helpful in contextualising objects. Ethnographic objects are all unique in terms of their manufacture, use and history. They are often items of exquisite workmanship and considerable beauty and are irreplaceable evidence of Scotland's contacts with the rest of the world.

The Collections Management Survey

An important objective of the Foreign Ethnographic Collections Research Programme was to assess how collections of foreign ethnography in Scotland are currently cared for, in order to assist museums to develop strategies for the management of these collections in the future. Some four hundred institutions and individual collectors were approached in the initial stage of the Programme to ascertain whether they had foreign ethnographic material. Fifty-three gave a positive response and agreed to participate in the Programme. Participant museums are listed in Part Two. Forty-five out of the fifty-three responded to the collections management survey. These may be grouped by managing authority as follows:

Local Authority	23
Independent	10
Regimental	4
Private	4
University	3
National	1

1 The museum's policy in respect of foreign ethnographic material in its care.

1.1 Does the collections management policy make reference to foreign ethnographic material? (private collections excluded)

Total respondents	41
Yes	17 (42%)
No	24 (58%)

1.2 Does the acquisition and disposal policy make specific reference to foreign ethnographic material? (private collections excluded)

Total respondents	41
Yes	22 (54%)
No	19 (46%)

1.3 Is there an acquisition budget specifically for foreign ethnographic material?

Total respondents	44
Yes	0
No	44 (100%)

For the purposes of the Museums and Galleries Commission Registration Scheme, a collections management policy is required to indicate, in summary form, what material is presently held in the collections. The policy should also include an acquisitions and disposal policy. Of the forty-one respondents, seventeen have collections management policies which make reference to their foreign ethnographic collections. Twenty-two make specific reference to this material in their acquisition and disposal policy. Twenty-four museums which have foreign ethnographic material make no reference to the material in their collections management policy document and fourteen do not refer to it in their acquisition and disposal policy.

There are four museums actively collecting foreign ethnography: the National Museums of Scotland, Glasgow Museums, the Hunterian Museum and Art Gallery and the Marischal Museum. The definition of collecting areas between museums is therefore only an issue between these four institutions. The majority of museums stated that they would refer potential donors to other more appropriate museums unless an item had strong local significance.

No museum has an acquisition budget solely for foreign ethnographic material. This is not to say that funds are not available. The National Museums of Scotland have purchase funds which are allocated according to departmental priorities, while the larger local authority museums have either a museum-wide allocation of funds or a system wherein individual requests are considered and must compete with other bids for funding. Foreign ethnographic material is eligible for support from the National Fund for Acquisitions, administered with Government funds by the National Museums of Scotland. For example, in 1990-91, the Hunterian Museum and Art Gallery and Glasgow Museums purchased items of foreign ethnography with support from the Fund. Further details of the Fund are available from the National Museums of Scotland. Information regarding allocations from the Fund is published in the Annual Report of the National Museums of Scotland.

It is recommended that collecting policies of museums should make specific reference to all material in their collections by including a comprehensive summary of collections in their collections policy document, irrespective of quantity, or whether the collection is little used at present. The Scottish Museums Council and the

Museums and Galleries Commission should encourage museums to pursue this.

2 The uses to which the museum puts its foreign ethnographic material.

2.1 Is the foreign ethnographic material used as an educational resource?

Total respondents	45
Yes	25 (56%)
No	20 (44%)

2.2 Is the foreign ethnographic material used in research?

Total respondents	45
Yes	35 (78%)
No	10 (22%)

2.3 Is it used in display?

Total respondents	45
Yes	32 (71%)
No	13 (29%)

2.4 Is it used for in-house exhibition?

Total respondents	45
Yes	18 (40%)
No	27 (60%)

2.5 Is foreign ethnographic material available for loan to external exhibitions (subject to conditions of loan)?

Total respondents	45
Yes	18 (40%)
No	27 (60%)

2.6 Does the museum/the owner receive enquiries about foreign ethnographic material?

Total respondents	45
Yes	17 (38%)
No	28 (62%)

2.7 Is there public access to the objects and any associated documentation (subject to conditions being met)?

Total respondents	45
Yes	35 (78%)
No	10 (22%)

As noted above, there is a variety of uses for foreign ethnographic material in a museum context. Fifty-six per cent of museums surveyed use this material as an educational resource, structured in some way, and available to organised school or adult learning groups. Forty-four per cent considered that their current use of material did not constitute educational use in these terms. However, 78% of collections (35 museums) had been used for research purposes either in-house or by others. Given the small size of the majority of collections in Scotland, this is encouraging. It is hoped that the findings of the Foreign Ethnographic Collections Research Programme and the creation of the National Database will facilitate further collections research.

The availability of foreign ethnographic material for loan may also be a reflection of the lack of specialist ethnographic curators, either to generate demand for incoming loans, or to service requests for outgoing loans. Although 40% of museums are willing to make their ethnographic material available for loan, this does not imply that approaches have been made to them.

The Museum Ethnographers Group was formed to promote the understanding of museum ethnography and encourage the exchange of information and resources between museum staff in the UK and abroad. Membership covers the whole range of museum personnel but is not exclusively drawn from museums. Personal and institutional membership is available. Museums and individuals with ethnography collections are encouraged to apply for membership of the Museum Ethnographers Group as a means of enhancing and updating their knowledge and use of ethnographic material through contact with other members and receipt of the *Journal of Museum Ethnography* and *MEG News*. A contact address for the Museum Ethnographers Group is given in Appendix 2.

The Scottish Museums Council's Museums Education Initiative is a three-year programme designed specifically to encourage museums and galleries of all types to provide increased educational support to schools. The Initiative has three aims:

1 To develop local projects with museums throughout Scotland, based on programmes of discovery and investigative learning across the curriculum.

2 To monitor the effectiveness of these projects, especially the changes in the patterns of educational use of museums and galleries as a result.

3 To encourage similar developments throughout

Scotland by practical example and by a publishing and marketing programme during and at the end of the Initiative.

It is recommended that museums with foreign ethnographic material plan to display their material and seek advice from specialist colleagues, representatives of cultural communities in the UK or nationals of countries from which the material originated.

It is recommended that museums with collections of foreign ethnography, whether or not they have dedicated staff, seek membership of the Museum Ethnographers Group as a means of enhancing and updating their knowledge and use of foreign ethnographic material through contact with other members and receipt of publications.

It is recommended that museums with foreign ethnographic material consider participating in the Museums Education Initiative to enhance the educational use of this rich resource of underused material.

3 Staffing.

3.1 Is there a qualified or experienced ethnography curator with designated responsibility for the foreign ethnographic material?

Total respondents	45
Yes	2 (4%)
No	43 (96%)

3.2 Is there a member of staff or an individual experienced or qualified in ethnography on the staff but with responsibilities other than for the foreign ethnographic material?

Total respondents	45
Yes	4 (9%)
No	41 (91%)

Glasgow Museums and the National Museums of Scotland have staff who are either qualified or experienced in foreign ethnography and are dedicated to the curation of foreign ethnographic material. The Hunterian Museum and Art Gallery, the Marischal Museum, the National Museums of Scotland and North East Fife District Museum Service have, at the time of writing, well-qualified or experienced ethnographers who have additional and wider responsibilities.

While only 9% of museums surveyed have qualified or experienced ethnography staff, 71% had foreign ethnographic material on display at the time of the survey. However, only 40% used material for short-term, in-

house, thematic exhibitions. It is suggested that while the lack of qualified or experienced ethnography staff may not deter museums from displaying material, it does affect the contextualised and interpretive use of the material in thematic temporary exhibitions and educational projects.

It is recommended that consideration be given to increased staffing:

a. There is a need for more dedicated posts in the museums with the largest collections.

b. Museums with larger collections should consider a pastoral role for their specialist staff on a cost-recoverable basis.

c. Museums with significant but numerically small collections which do not justify specialist posts might wish to collaborate in the appointment of a dedicated curator to cover several museum collections which are geographically close, such as in the West of Scotland.

4 The plans for the future regarding foreign ethnographic material in the museum or collection.

4.1 Are there any future plans for the foreign ethnographic material?

Total respondents	45
Positive	24 (53%)
Status quo	20 (45%)
Transfer	1 (2%)

4.2 Has de-accessioning the material been considered?

Total respondents	45
Yes	4 (9%)
No	41 (91%)

4.3 Has the transfer of foreign ethnographic material been considered?

Total respondents	45
Yes	8 (18%)
No	37 (82%)

At the time of the survey, 24 museums (53%) had positive plans for the development of their ethnographic collections. Plans included accessioning, retrospective accessioning, collections research, upgrading documentation, display and increased use in student teaching. For example, Dundee Art Galleries and Museums is planning a project which will build on the findings of the Programme, enhance documentation and will further improve standards of care and interpretation. The Marischal Museum is concerned to make greater use of material culture in student teaching. North East Scotland Museums Service is seeking to display more of its collections, has a preventive conservation programme which includes the ethnographic collection, and aims to enhance standards of care. Forty-five per cent of museums had no plans to implement new projects. One institution may transfer material as it no longer has a museum function or curatorial staff.

It is recommended that all museums with foreign ethnographic material include this specifically in the Forward Planning process.

It is recommended that museums considering the disposal of foreign ethnographic material adhere to the guidelines issued by the Museums and Galleries Commission in its Registration Scheme for museums.

It is recommended that museums planning the disposal of foreign ethnographic material consider transferring it to other museums with appropriate collections in Scotland.

5 Collections Care.

A Collections Care Guide developed for use in a survey of industrial and social history collections in Yorkshire and Humberside museums (Kenyon, 1992) was taken as a basis for measuring and comparing the physical conditions in the museums surveyed. The standards used were initially devised for industrial and social history collections but were considered equally applicable to the storage of foreign ethnographic material.

Figure 4 presents the criteria and requirements graded A to E. 'A' represents the optimum standard and 'E' completely unacceptable. 'C' is set as the minimum acceptable standard and relates to the basic requirements of the Museums and Galleries Commission's Registration Scheme.

Figures 5 and 6 present the findings of the collections care aspect of the Collections Management Survey.

Results relate to areas in which ethnographic material is stored (not displayed). They do not necessarily reflect conditions pertaining to other collections held unless they share the same storage areas.

From Figure 5 it can be seen that the following percentages of museums achieved or surpassed the minimum acceptable standard (C) in each category :

Environment	36%
Light	68%
Cleanliness	59%
General storage	57%

However, it is clear that a number of museums are having difficulty, particularly in respect of environmental standards.

In *A Conservation Survey of Museum Collections in Scotland* (Ramer, 1989), Ramer defined the basic needs of the ethnographic collections surveyed at that time as being 'the establishment of regular programmes of environmental monitoring ... the upgrading of storage arrangements, involving the reorganisation of available spaces, the repacking of packed items using stable materials, and the provision of dust covers for items not kept in containers'. Ramer also noted the need for the provision of remedial conservation treatment.

In 1993, the Scottish Museums Council followed up the Ramer study with *An Evaluation of the Conservation Needs of Museum Collections in Scotland* (Slade, 1993). 'Examination of the responses received in the evaluation study reveals that there has been very little improvement in the care of ethnographic collections and that very few of the recommendations made in the site surveys have been acted upon.' Slade recommends that priority should be given to arranging visits from the Scottish Museums Council's Conservation Service Manager. These should be followed up with financial assistance for specialist assessments and any urgently required preventive conservation improvements, following on from the findings of the Foreign Ethnographic Collections Research Programme.

The Collections Management Survey undertaken for this Programme is a 'snapshot' of the situation in each museum. As the case-study on Paisley Museum and Art Galleries exemplifies (p 12), there has already been positive action in this direction in some museums which have participated in the Foreign Ethnographic Collections Research Programme in response to a visit and recommendations made by the Council's Conservation Service Manager.

It is recommended that the Scottish Museums Council seeks specific funding for the care of foreign ethnographic collections within its Conservation Initiative and encourages a positive response to the recommendations made in the *Evaluation of the Conservation Needs of Museum Collections in Scotland* (Slade, 1993) which this report endorses.

Figure 4: Collections Management Criteria and Requirements

	Collections Well Managed		Acceptable Standard	Collections at Risk	
	A	**B**	**C**	**D**	**E**
Environment	Monitoring Air conditioned Stable	Controllable heating Humidifiers/ De-humidifiers Monitoring Stable	Monitoring Relatively stable within acceptable limits	No monitoring No visible deterioration of objects	Fluctuation Problems (eg leaks, damp)
Light	No daylight Monitoring Control by other means (eg blinds, curtains) Filters	Some daylight Monitoring Control by other means (eg blinds, curtains) Filters	Daylight No monitoring Control by other means (eg blinds, curtains) Filters	Daylight No monitoring No control No filters	Substantial daylight No monitoring No control No filters Sensitive items at risk
Cleanliness	Regular cleaning Dust prevention Programmed checking of items	Regular cleaning Dust prevention (eg dust sheet, filter)	Regular cleaning Anti-dust measures (eg floor coverings)	Dusty Poor dust resistance Inadequate floor covering	Filthy Neglected
General Storage	Racks Boxes Boxes labelled by subject and item Handlists Access good Handling area	Racks Boxes labelled by subject and items Small overspill to floor Access good	Racking Boxes labelled by subject Large overspill to floor Reasonable access	Partially racked Boxes Access poor Damage to objects may occur	No racks No boxes Access very difficult Objects at risk

Figure 4: Collections Management Criteria and Requirements

	Optimum	Minimum		Unacceptable	
Scores	**A**	**B**	**C**	**D**	**E**
Total Respondents	44	44	44	44	44
Environment	1 (2%)	7 (16%)	8 (18%)	18 (41%)	10 (23%)
Light level	0	6 (14%)	24 (54%)	8 (18%)	6 (14%)
Cleanliness	0	2 (5%)	24 (54%)	15 (34%)	3 (7%)
General Storage	2 (5%)	6 (14%)	17 (38%)	10 (23%)	9 (20%)

Figure 5: Collections Care Scores

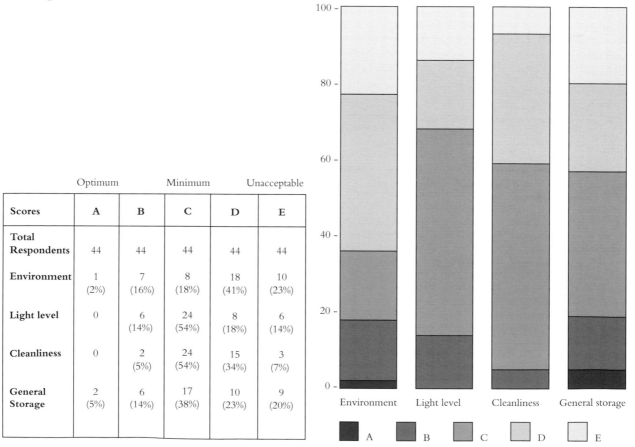

Figure 6: Collections Management Findings

The Next Steps

Timothy Ambrose

Introduction

This section of the report examines how the Scottish Museums Council can support museums and their governing bodies in responding to the findings and recommendations given above.

The report has not only identified what foreign ethnographic material exists in Scottish museums and collections, but has also explored how that material is managed and used by those responsible for it. It is clear that in many instances foreign ethnographic material is well looked after and imaginatively used in displays, exhibitions, and education programmes. However, as the report makes clear, there are significant opportunities for improving standards of care and use. Both curators and governing bodies of museums should be aware of how the care and use of their foreign ethnographic collections can be improved and developed.

The Scottish Museums Council is able to provide a range of support to those member museums who wish to develop a management strategy based on the findings of this report. There are four main areas in which necessary improvements have been identified: conservation, both preventive and remedial; research and scholarship; documentation and usage. In each of these areas there are different ways in which the Council can help museums, through advisory and information services, training, remedial conservation, grant-aid, advocacy, and fundraising.

Conservation

The Scottish Museums Council places a high priority on the care and conservation of collections of all types. Foreign ethnographic collections have particular conservation needs and it is important for museums to recognise their particularly vulnerable nature. Many items are very fragile and made from organic materials. In some cases, transient elements (traces of substances used in ritual for example) exist on objects. Ethnographic material such as grass skirts and baskets is easily damaged beyond repair by inappropriate environmental conditions such as excessive dryness, damp and dirt, or by poor storage and handling.

To help museums with ethnographic collections, the Council provides information, training and advice on preventive conservation, in particular, the appropriate packing and storage of items, and the environmental conditions under which they should be stored and displayed. This is a particularly important area of the Council's work and general advisory services are provided to both full and associate members of the Council. Where there is a need for more specialised advice on preventive conservation, for example from a specialist conservator, then full members of the Council who are registered under the Museums and Galleries Commission's national Museum Registration Scheme are eligible for grant-aid support to help meet the costs. Where detailed advice is given to a museum, a report on preventive conservation improvements is prepared to provide guidance in its forward planning for the short, medium and long-term. The conservation report and the museum's forward plan, identifying programmes of positive action, can also be used to support applications for financial assistance to external agencies where appropriate.

The Scottish Museums Council can also provide help to museums where there is a need for remedial conservation. The Council's conservation service is able to provide remedial conservation services for foreign ethnographic material to its member museums. Full members of the Council who are registered are eligible for grant-aid support for remedial conservation work carried out by the Council's own conservation service. Where another conservation service which has been approved by the Council is used, members are also eligible for financial support. The Council works closely with the Scottish Conservation Bureau and the Museums and Galleries Commission's Conservation Unit. Their respective Conservation Registers provide information about appropriate conservators available to undertake remedial conservation work on foreign ethnographic material and museums are able to request information from these sources if necessary. Relevant addresses are given in Appendix 2.

Before any remedial conservation is undertaken, the museum should have had a conservation survey of its ethnographic collections carried out by a specialist conservator to identify conservation priorities. These should be matched to curatorial priorities and a programme of remedial work then identified and integrated into the museum's forward plan. A museum may wish to contract external curatorial support where there is no in-house specialist. Where a museum requires additional specialist curatorial advice in this process to complement or extend the findings of the Programme, this is also eligible for grant-aid assistance from the Council.

The Council's *Conservation Initiative - A Future for Scotland's Past* provides additional funding for remedial and preventive conservation programmes for foreign ethnographic material to complement its existing grant-aid programmes. Details of the Conservation Initiative's funds can be obtained from the Council's offices.

Control Of Substances Hazardous to Health (COSHH)

One of the issues which arose from the Foreign Ethnographic Collections Research Programme was that of health and safety when dealing with foreign ethnographic collections. The organic nature of many items means that they are not only vulnerable to adverse environmental conditions, such as insect attack and mould, but also liable to harbour residues or insects which can have an adverse effect on the health of researchers or museum staff. Every care needs to be taken in the context of the Control of Substances Hazardous to Health Regulations (1988), to ensure that these issues are recognised in the care and management of foreign ethnographic collections, and that appropriate steps are taken to protect museum staff or researchers in their handling and use of collections.

Research and Scholarship

The Programme has shown the value and benefits of carrying out detailed collections research. In many instances, it has provided, for the first time, detailed specialist advice to museum curators responsible for foreign ethnographic material. This specialist research work has given museums a closer understanding of the historical significance of items in their care; increased opportunities to compare material from one museum collection to another; created information resources which can be used for future exhibitions, displays and publications; provided the basis for improved multicultural understanding; illustrated the educational potential of ethnographic collections in terms of the new Scottish curricula, and demonstrated how Scots through the centuries have been involved with, and recorded their interest in, countries around the world. The research has therefore provided many durable benefits which can improve the abilities of museums to serve their various public audiences.

However, there is still a significant amount of research to be carried out to enhance the quality of information held by museums about their ethnographic collections. Such work can extend the range of information and improve public access to this remarkable resource.

There is much of value that can be done by museum staff at a local level in researching collections, and the Programme data held by the National Museums of Scotland National Database can support this activity through, for example, the reconstitution of collections split between different museums. There may, however, be a need for continued specialist research in certain areas or on certain collections. The employment of additional specialist consultants to provide more detailed reports on collections or aspects of collections is eligible for grant-aid support for full members of the Council with registered status.

In some cases it may be appropriate for a group of museums to engage a specialist consultant to provide a follow-up report to the initial work of the Programme, where, for example, an exhibition or an educational pack is being developed. Such projects are also eligible for grant-aid support from the Council.

Documentation

There is a considerable amount of additional work to be carried out by museums both in primary documentation and enhancement of existing collections documentation. Advisory services in documentation are provided by the National Museums of Scotland Scottish Museums Documentation Service which works in close liaison with the Scottish Museums Council in providing support to museums throughout Scotland. Where museums are eligible for these services, they should contact the Scottish Museums Documentation Officer at the National Museums of Scotland to discuss availability of support. Where advisory staff recommend improvements to documentation systems, such as computers and software development, museums eligible for Scottish Museums Council grant-aid may wish to apply for financial assistance to help implement the recommendations of the advisory reports. Training Services in documentation are provided through the Scottish Museums Council's training programme in conjunction with the Museum Documentation Association and the National Museums of Scotland.

The Programme provides a considerable range of information which will assist museums in the development of their collections documentation. One of its strengths is the opportunity provided to compare collections from one museum to another and to identify collections which feature in more than one museum. It is possible, therefore, to identify more accurately than ever before the significance of particular collections. This allows museums to enhance their collections documentation through the addition of new information and to argue for additional resources for the management of their collections in the light of their relative importance.

Collections usage

There are some 53 institutions in Scotland which hold foreign ethnographic collections. These museums have employed their ethnographic collections in a variety of ways in the past on an individual or joint basis, in displays, exhibitions, educational programmes, and leisure learning programmes. The Programme has examined, through its field-work, the range of usage of foreign ethnographic collections made by museums. It is clear that despite some exciting recent programmes and developments, those mentioned in Part Three for instance, many other opportunities exist to use foreign ethnographic collections to extend audience interest and to justify their continued curatorship.

The Scottish Museums Council's Leisure Learning Programme demonstrated the value of imaginative informal learning programmes based on collections of different types to extend audience interest at all ages in the work of museums. The Council continues to provide advice, information and financial support to museums establishing leisure learning programmes to assist in their marketing (Stewart, 1989). As we have noted, foreign ethnographic collections could be used more extensively and more imaginatively in developing new audiences for museums in Scotland. *Presenting Other Cultures* provides a range of ideas and examples for their more effective use within leisure learning programmes.

The Programme also draws attention to the opportunities for formal education programmes presented by foreign ethnographic collections. The Museums Education Initiative of the Scottish Museums Council has been established to examine how museums can most effectively relate their work to the needs of the 5-14 syllabus and Standard Grade. Foreign ethnographic collections provide a rich resource for underpinning the new curricula, and museums which wish to use their collections in this way can look to the Scottish Museums Council for advice and financial support to assist their work.

The development and renewal of displays in museums is another area in which the Scottish Museums Council can assist museums eligible for financial support. Changing methods of interpretation and presentation of foreign ethnographic collections, and the ethical considerations which accompany the display of cultural material, mean that many museums are reappraising their approaches to display. Published information on new developments in the use and care of foreign ethnographic collections at UK and international level is available through the Scottish Museums Council's Information Services, in particular its monthly information service, *Museum Abstracts*.

Forward Planning

The Foreign Ethnographic Collections Research Programme demonstrates the need for museums with foreign ethnographic collections to include their care and use in their forward planning, (Ambrose and Runyard, 1991). There is a need to include foreign ethnographic collections in collections management planning, but it is also important for museums to build foreign ethnographic collections into other areas of forward planning such as education and leisure learning. Advice on forward planning for museums may be obtained through the Scottish Museums Council's advisory services and training programmes.

PART IV:
SUMMARY AND
RECOMMENDATIONS

Summary

Background

The collections of foreign ethnography included in this survey originate from Africa, Oceania, Asia and the Americas. The variety of artefacts included within them is very large, ranging from everyday objects such as tools and domestic utensils to religious and ceremonial items such as masks and sculpture. The specialised knowledge required to interpret such collections is often lacking, especially in small museums, and this has led to neglect and under-resourcing of an irreplaceable archive of material.

The Foreign Ethnographic Collections Research Programme was devised to assist museums in improving the quality of care and use of such collections by recording their existence. The two-year programme, managed by the Scottish Museums Council and the National Museums of Scotland in association with the University of Glasgow, was funded by the Economic and Social Research Council, award number R00232461.

Programme Objectives

1 To establish the location of foreign ethnographic collections in museums, universities, research institutes and private collections in Scotland.

2 To encourage and coordinate the recording of information about foreign ethnographic collections by in-house museum staff.

3 To record collections or organise recording by other specialists in cases where no professional staff are available to undertake the work.

4 To encourage comparative research on key items and collections for publication.

5 To establish a computerised database for the recorded information and to publish the findings of the survey programme.

The dissemination of findings will be to research workers in the field and to museums and allied institutions for use in their collections management and for public exhibitions or similar purposes.

Results of the Programme

The Foreign Ethnographic Collections National Database

The major outcome is the creation of an extensive database of almost 90,000 foreign ethnographic artefacts held in 53 collections in Scotland. The database, part of the National Museums of Scotland National Database development, is established as an important research tool. This book provides a point of entry into the database by means of a summary catalogue organised by broad geographical area and explains how museums can enhance standards of care and presentation for their foreign ethnographic collections.

The Collections Management Survey

In addition to creating the National Database a collections management survey was undertaken, addressing five main issues:

1 The museum's policy in respect of foreign ethnographic material in its care.

2 The uses to which the museum puts its collection.

3 Staffing of collections.

4 Plans for the future use of the collection.

5 Physical care of the collections.

Of the 53 museums with foreign ethnographic material, 45 responded to the collections management survey. The results indicate that, while museums have responded to the need to devise policy in respect of management and care of their collections generally, a significant number have overlooked the need to make specific reference to foreign ethnographic material. Despite the lack of formal policy, foreign ethnographic collections are widely used in research and long-term display, although use requiring specialist ethnographic knowledge, such as temporary thematic exhibitions, is less extensive. Few museums have qualified or experienced ethnography curators. There is room for improvement in the forward planning of management and use of foreign ethnographic collections, and collections care is in need of serious attention and resourcing.

Recommendations

1 Collecting policies of museums should make specific reference to all material in their collections by including a comprehensive summary of collections in their collections policy document, irrespective of quantity, or whether the collection is little used at present. The Scottish Museums Council and the Museums and Galleries Commission should encourage museums to pursue this.

2 Museums with foreign ethnographic material should plan to display their material and seek advice from specialist colleagues, representatives of cultural communities in the UK or nationals of countries from which the material originated.

3 Museums with collections of foreign ethnography, whether or not they have dedicated staff, should seek membership of the Museum Ethnographers Group as a means of enhancing and updating their knowledge and use of foreign ethnographic material through contact with other members and receipt of publications.

4 Museums with foreign ethnographic material should consider participating in the Scottish Museum Council's Education Initiative to enhance the educational use of this rich resource of underused material.

5 Consideration should be given to increased staffing:

a There is a need for more dedicated posts in the museums with the largest collections.
b Museums with larger collections should consider a pastoral role for their specialist staff on a cost-recoverable basis.
c Museums with significant but numerically small collections which do not justify specialist posts might wish to collaborate in the appointment of a dedicated curator to cover several museum collections which are geographically close, such as in the West of Scotland.

6 Museums with foreign ethnographic material should include this specifically in the forward planning process.

7 Museums considering the disposal of foreign ethnographic material should adhere to the guidelines issued by the Museums and Galleries Commission in its Registration Scheme for museums.

8 Museums planning the disposal of foreign ethnographic material should consider transferring it to other museums with appropriate collections in Scotland.

9 The Scottish Museums Council should seek specific funding for the care of foreign ethnographic collections within its Conservation Initiative and encourage a positive response to the recommendations made in the *Evaluation of the Conservation Needs of Museum Collections in Scotland* (Slade, 1993) which this report endorses.

Appendices

Appendix 1: References

Ambrose, T and S Runyard, (eds). *Forward Planning: A handbook of business, corporate, and development planning for museums and galleries*. London: Museums & Galleries Commission/Routledge, 1991.

Drysdale, L. *A World of Learning: University Collections in Scotland*. Edinburgh: HMSO, 1990.

Evaluating Artefacts. Leicester: Centre for Multicultural Education, Leicester/Leicestershire Museums Arts and Records Service, n.d.

GB: Health & Safety Executive. *Control of Substances Hazardous to Health* Regulations 1988. London: HSE, 1990.

Kenyon, J. *Collecting for the 21st Century: a survey of industrial and social history collections in the museums of Yorkshire and Humberside*. Leeds: Yorkshire & Humberside Museums Council, 1992.

McCorry, H C. Bad Language in Ethnography Records. *Museum Management and Curatorship* 10 (4), 1991, 433–434.

Museum Abstracts. Edinburgh: Scottish Museums Council.

Museum Ethnographers Group. *Journal of Museum Ethnography*. Hull, 1989-.

Museums and Galleries Commission. *Museums in Scotland: Report by a Working Party*. HMSO, 1986.

Museums Yearbook. London: Museums Association.

Ramer, B. *A Conservation Survey of Museum Collections in Scotland*. Edinburgh, 1989.

Schumann, Y. *Museum Ethnographers Group Survey of Ethnographic Collections in the United Kingdom, Eire and the Channel Islands: Interim Report*. Hull, 1986.

Stewart, D. *Building New Audiences for Museums* (VHS Video). Edinburgh: HMSO/Scottish Museums Council, 1989.

Appendix 2: Resources

Museums in Scotland with specialist foreign ethnography curators:

Glasgow Museums
Kelvingrove
Glasgow G3 8AG

Hunterian Museum and Art Gallery
The University
Glasgow G12 8QQ

Marischal Museum
Marischal College
University of Aberdeen
Aberdeen AB9 1AS

National Museums of Scotland
Chambers Street
Edinburgh EH1 1JF

Other museums in the UK with specialist foreign ethnography curators:

Birmingham Museum and Art Gallery
Chamberlain Square
Birmingham B3 3DH

Brighton Art Gallery and Museum
Church Street
Brighton BN1 1UE

The Horniman Museum and Library
London Road
Forest Hill
London SE23 3PQ

Leeds City Museum
Municipal Buildings
Calverley Street
Leeds LS1 3AA

The Manchester Museum
The University of Manchester
Oxford Road
Manchester M13 9PL

The Museum of Mankind
(Ethnography Department of the British Museum)

6 Burlington Gardens
London W1X 2EX

Pitt Rivers Museum
University of Oxford
Parks Road
Oxford OX1 3PP

Saffron Walden Museum
Museum Street
Saffron Walden
Essex CB10 1JL

Ulster Museum
Botanic Gardens
Belfast BT9 5AB

University Museum of Archaeology and
Anthropology
Downing Street
Cambridge CB2 3EQ

**Enquiries regarding the Museum Ethnographers
Group should be addressed to:**

The Secretary
MEG
University Museum of Archaeology and Anthropology
Downing Street
Cambridge CB2 3DZ

for membership subscriptions

Mrs Margret Carey
MEG Treasurer
2 Frank Dixon Way
London SE21 7BB

**Information regarding appropriate conservators in
the private sector may be obtained from the following:**

Scottish Conservation Bureau
3 Stenhouse Mill Lane
Edinburgh EH11 3LR
Telephone: 031 443 1666

Conservation Unit
Museums and Galleries Commission
16 Queen Anne's Gate
London SW1H 9AA
Telephone: 071 233 3683 (Conservation Register
enquiries only)

There is a nominal charge for non-members of a UK
Area Museum Council seeking information from the
Conservation Register maintained by the Museums and
Galleries Commission Conservation Unit.

Appendix 3: Bibliographies
The Care of Ethnographic Collections

Conservation of Ethnographic Materials Occasional Paper
No. 1, Ipswich: Museum Ethnographers Group, 1982.

Cranstone, B A L. *Ethnography*. Handbook for Museum
Curators Series, London: Museums Association, 1958.

Ramer, B. *A Conservation Survey of Museum Collections in
Scotland*. Edinburgh: Scottish Museums Council, 1989.

Slade, S. *An Evaluation of the Conservation Needs of
Museum Collections in Scotland*. Edinburgh: Scottish
Museums Council, 1993.

Assistance in the Identification of Collections of
Foreign Ethnography

There are few well-illustrated general books on foreign
ethnography. Many of the most useful are out of print
and can be obtained only from specialist book dealers or
through inter-library loan. Museums with large collections of foreign ethnography and qualified or experienced staff normally have specialist libraries which may
be consulted by appointment (see museums listed
above). The following bibliography is selected on the
basis of those books and articles which ethnographers on
the Management Committee have found most useful in
helping to identify items in collections. They all include
further bibliographies.

General

*The British Museum Handbook to the Ethnographic
Collections*. London, (1910), 1925.

Jenkins, J. *Musical Instruments*. London: Horniman
Museum, 1958.

   Man & Music. Edinburgh: Royal Scottish
Museum, 1983.

Phelps, S. *Art and Artefacts of the Pacific, Africa and the
Americas, The James Hooper Collection*. London, 1976.

Stone, G. *Glossary of Arms and Armour*. London, (1930),
1961.

Africa

Carey, M. *Beads and Beadwork of West and Central Africa*.
Princes Risborough: Shire Publications, 1991.

   Beads and Beadwork of East and Central Africa.
Princes Risborough: Shire Publications, 1991.

Fischer, W and M Zirngibl. *African Weapons: Knives,*

Daggers, Swords, Axes, Throwing Knives. Passau, 1978.
Picton, J and J Mack. *African Textiles*. London: British Museum, (1979), 1989.

Sieber, R. *African Furniture and Household Objects*. New York: American Federation of Arts, 1980.

Zirngibl, M. *Rare African Short Weapons*. Grafenau, 1983.

Americas

The Spirit Sings: Artistic Traditions of Canada's First Peoples, A Catalogue of the Exhibition. Toronto, 1987.

Birket-Smith, K. *The Eskimos*. London, 1926.

Bushnell, G H S. *Ancient Arts of the Americas*. London, (1965), 1967.

Coe, R T. *Sacred Circles: Two Thousand Years of North American Indian Art*. London, 1976.

Feest, C F. *Native Arts of North America*. London, 1980.

Lowie, R H. *Indians of the Plains*. 1963.

Pearce, S M. *Towards the Pole: a Catalogue of the Eskimo Collections*. City of Exeter Museums and Art Gallery, Publication 82, 1976.

Asia
China

Garner, H. *Chinese Lacquer*. London, 1979.

Kerr, R. *Chinese Ceramics, Porcelain of the Qing Dynasty 1644-1911*. London: Victoria & Albert Museum, 1986.

Medley, M. *The Chinese Potter*. Oxford, 1976.

Tregear, M. *Chinese Art*. London, 1980.

Wilson, V. *Chinese Dress*. London: Victoria & Albert Museum, 1990.

Japan

Bushell, R. *The Inro Handbook, Studies of Netsuke, Inro and Lacquer*. New York, 1979.

Harris, V and N Ogasawara. *Swords of the Samurai*. London: British Museum, 1990.

Jenyns, S. *Japanese Porcelain*. London, 1965.

Japanese Pottery. London, 1971.

Smith, L, V Harris and T Clark. *Japanese Art: Masterpieces in the British Museum*. London, 1990.

Watson, W (ed). *The Great Japan Exhibition, Art of the Edo Period 1600-1868*. London, 1990.

India

Birdwood, George C M. *The Industrial Arts of India*. London, (1880), 1971.

Blurton, T Richard. *Hindu Art*. London: British Museum, 1992.

Guy, J and D Swallow. *Arts of India 1550-1900*. London: Victoria & Albert Museum, 1990.

Tibet

Pott, P H. *Introduction to the Tibetan Collection of the National Museums of Ethnology*. Leiden, 1951.

Middle East

Brend, B. *Islamic Art*. London: British Museum, 1991.

Lane, A. *Later Islamic Pottery*. London, 1971.

Melikian-Chirvani, A S. *Islamic Metalwork from the Iranian World*. London: Victoria & Albert Museum, 1982.

Wurff, Hans E. *The Traditional Crafts of Persia*. Cambridge (Mass), 1966.

Oceania

Barrow, T. *Art and Life in Polynesia*. London, 1971.

Maori Art of New Zealand. Paris, 1978.

Clunie, F. *Fijian Weapons and Warfare*. Bulletin of the Fiji Museum, 2, 1977.

Cranstone, B A L. *Melanesia: A Short Ethnography*. London: British Museum, 1961.

The Australian Aborigines. London: British Museum, 1973.

Collections of Foreign Ethnography in Scotland

Adamson, H. A Carved Wooden Figure from Easter Island. *Scottish Art Review* XI (1), 1967, 24.

Aldred, C. A Tauihi and Two Taurapa. *Scottish Art Review* VIII (1), 1961, 26-29.

Archey, G. *The Art Forms of Polynesia*. Bull. 4, Auckland, 1965.

Arts of Asia. Special issue on the Oriental Collections in the Burrell Collection: Glasgow, 20 (3).

Barrow, T. Free-standing Maori Images. In J D Freeman and W R Geddes (eds). *Anthropology in the South Seas*. New Plymouth, New Zealand: Thomas Avery and Sons, 1959, 111-120.

Art and Life in Polynesia. London, 1971.

The Art of Tahiti. London, 1979.

Bassani, E and W B Fagg. *Africa & the Renaissance: Art in Ivory*. New York, 1988.

Brincard, M (ed). *Sounding Forms: African Musical Instruments*. New York, 1989.

Brock, C H. Dr Hunter's South Seas Curiosities. *Scottish Art Review* XV (2), 1973, 6-9, 37-39.

Buck, P H. *Arts and Crafts of the Cook Islands*. Honolulu: Bernice P Bishop Museum, Bull. 179, 1944.

Burland, C A. An Oil-lacquered Gourd from Ancient Mexico. *Scottish Art Review* VII (2), 1959, 26-27.

Burnham, D K. *To Please the Caribou*. Toronto, 1992.

Bushnell, G H S. Peruvian Textiles in the Burrell Collection. *Scottish Art Review* VIII (1), 1961, 22-25.

Coe, R T. *Sacred Circles:Two Thousand Years of North American Art*. London, 1976.

The Spirit Sings, Artistic Traditions of Canada's First Peoples, A Catalogue of the Exhibition Toronto, 1987.

Craw-Eismont, B. *A Brief History of the North American Ethnography Collections in Six Scottish Museums.* Unpublished M.Litt, University of St Andrews, 1992.

Dark, P J C. Two bronze heads from Benin. *Scottish Art Review* VIII (1), 1961, 5-11.

Farmer, G H. Some Oriental Instruments at Kelvingrove. *Scottish Art Review* VIII (1), 1961 1-4.

Feest, C F. *Native Arts of North America*. London, 1980.

Gower, T. *Art of the Mende from Sierra Leone. The Guy Massie-Taylor Collection*. Glasgow: Glasgow Museums and Art Galleries, 1980.

Gustafson, P. *Salish Weaving*. Vancouver, 1980.

Haddon, A C. and J Hornell. *Canoes of Oceania*. (2 vols), Honolulu: Bernice P Bishop Museum, Special Publication 27, 1936.

Hannah, A. Chinese Pottery and Porcelain in the Burrell Collection. *Scottish Art Review* II (4), 1949, 16-20.

Henderson, S M K. African Masks and Sculpture. *Scottish Art Review* I (2), 1946, 14-16, 28-29.

Hitchcock, M. *Indonesian Textile Techniques*. Princes Risborough: Shire Publications, 1985.

Holm, B. A Wooling Mantle Neatly Wrought: The Early Historic Record of Northwest Coast Patterned-Twined Textiles – 1784-1850. *American Indian Art Magazine* 8 (1), Winter 1982, 34-47.

Hunt, C. The Exotic Heritage. *Deeside Field* 17, 1981.
Shark Tooth and Stone Blade. Catalogue of the Pacific art in the University of Aberdeen, 1981.

The Anthropological Museum-Past and Future. *Aberdeen University Review*, 1984.

Alexander Thomson - Gentleman and Collector. *Deeside Field* 18, 1985.

African Art in Aberdeen. *African Arts* 19 (4), 1986.

The Elepe's beadwork: a question of legitimacy. In S Pearce (ed), *Museum Economics and the Community*. Athlone Press, 1991, 177-191.

Taonga Maori in the University of Aberdeen. *Proceedings of the Taonga Maori Conference*. Wellington, New Zealand, November 1990, 152-158.

Hutchings, R. Designs on Australian Aboriginal Shields and Boomerangs. *Scottish Art Review* IX (3), 1964, 23-25, 30.

Idiens, D. *Traditional African Sculpture in the Royal Scottish Museum*. Edinburgh: HMSO, 1969.

Ancient American Art in the Royal Scottish Museum. Edinburgh: HMSO, 1971.

The Athapaskans: Strangers of the North. Ottawa: National Museum of Man, 1974 (part author).

A Catalogue of Northern Athapaskan Indian Artefacts in the Collection of the Royal Scottish Museum. Edinburgh: HMSO, 1979.

An Introduction to Traditional African Weaving and Textiles. *Textile History* 11, 1980, 5-21.

The Hausa of Northern Nigeria: A Catalogue of the R E Miller Collection and others in the Royal Scottish Museum. Edinburgh: HMSO, 1981.

Pacific Art in the Royal Scottish Museum. Edinburgh: HMSO, 1982.

A Catalogue of the Ethnographic Collections: Oceania, America, Africa. Perth: Perth Art Gallery and Museum, 1983.

A Catalogue of Ethnographic Boat Models in the Royal Scottish Museum. Edinburgh: HMSO, 1984.

New Benin Discoveries in Scotland. *African Arts* 19 (4), August 1986, 52.

Northwest Coast Artefacts in Perth Museum and Art Gallery: The Colin Robertson Collection. *American Indian Art Magazine* 13 (1), Winter 1987, 46-74.
Eskimos in Scotland c.1682-1924. In C F Feest (ed), *Indians and Europe, An Interdisciplinary Collection of Essays.* Aachen: Edition Herodot, Raderverlag Forum II, 1987, 161-74.

Cook Islands Art. Princes Risborough: Shire Publications, 1990.

Chipewyan Artefacts collected by Robert Campbell and others in the National Museums of Scotland. In P A McCormack and R Geoffrey Ironside (eds), *Proceedings of the Fort Chipewyan and Fort Vermilion Bicentennial Conference.* University of Alberta, Edmonton, 1990, 278-280.

A case study in redefining the criteria for collecting African artefacts: the National Museums of Scotland. *Art in Africa 2: Collecting, Documenting, Preserving, Restoring and Exhibiting African Traditional Art.* Centro di Study di Storia delle Arti Africane, Florence, 1991, 70-77.

Rae and the Native Canadians and Rae as Collector and Ethnographer, in *No Ordinary Journey, John Rae Arctic Explorer 1813-1893.* Edinburgh and Toronto, 1993, 67-112.

Jacobs, J. African Art at the Glasgow Art Gallery and Museum. *African Arts* 19 (2), 1986, 28-40, 90.

Ethnography. *Glasgow Art Gallery and Museum.* London and Glasgow: Collins, 1987, 50-56.

Jenkins, J. *Man and Music.* Edinburgh: Royal Scottish Museum, 1983.

Kaeppler, A. *Artificial Curiosities.* Honolulu: Bernice P Bishop Museum, Special Publication 65, 1978.

Kissell, M L. Organised Salish Blanket Patterns. *American Anthropologist* NS 31, 1921, 85-88, 14C.

Korea Foundation *The Korean Relics in Western Europe.* Korea, 1992.

Lindsay, T B. Basketry and Weaving of the North Pacific Coast. *Scottish Art Review* VIII (1), 1961, 16-21.

Lovelace, A J. The African Collections at Glasgow Art Gallery and Museum. *Journal of Museum Ethnography* 3, 1991, 15-30.

Making Local Collections. Collecting in the Context of a Multicultural Exhibition. *Journal of Museum Ethnography* 3, 1991, 88-104.

Art for Industry, The Glasgow Japan Exchange of 1878. Glasgow Museums, 1991.

The Pacific Collections at Glasgow Art Gallery and Museum. *Pacific Arts* 5, 1992, 19-23.

Lovelace A J. and N Pearce. Islamic Material at Glasgow Museums. *Arts and The Islamic World* 19, 95-104.

McCormack, P A. *Northwind Dreaming: Fort Chipewyan,1788-1988.* Provincial Museum of Alberta, Special Publication 6, 1988.

Mackie, E W. William Hunter and Captain Cook: the 18th-century Ethnographical Collections in the Hunterian Museum. *Glasgow Archaeological Journal* 12, 1985, 1-18.

Reynolds, B Beothuk. *Handbook of North American Indians* 15, North East, William C Sturtevent (series ed), Washington, 1987, 101-108.

Roth, H Ling *The Maori Mantle.* Halifax, 1923.

Scarce, J M. Album paintings of Wen-Cheng Ming. *Burlington Magazine* 109, 1967, 417.

A problem piece of Kashmiri metalwork. *Iran* (Journal of the British Institute of Persian Studies), 1971, 71-85.

A Persian brassière. *AARP* (Art and Archaeology Research Papers) 7, 1975, 15-21.

The development of women's veils in Persia and Afghanistan. *Costume* (The Journal of the Costume Society) 9, 1975, 4-14.

Ali Mohammad Isfahani, tile-maker of Tehran. *Oriental Art* (New Series) 22, 1976, 278-288.

Turkish fashion in transition. *Costume* 14, 1980.

Middle Eastern Costume - from the tribes and cities of Iran and Turkey. Edinburgh: Royal Scottish Museum, 1981, 1-40.
Yuan and Ming lacquers in the Royal Scottish Museum, Edinburgh. In W Watson (ed), *Lacquer work in*

Asia and beyond. Colloquies on Art and Archaeology in Asia 11, Percival David Foundation of Chinese Art, University of London,1982.

Coptic and early Islamic Textiles. Edinburgh: Royal Scottish Museum, 1982.

Embroidery and lace of Ottoman Turkey. Edinburgh: Royal Scottish Museum, 1983.

Karagoz shadow puppets of Turkey. Edinburgh: Royal Scottish Museum, 1983.

Indian women from village and city 1850-1960. Edinburgh: Royal Scottish Museum, 1984.

Das osmanisch-turkische Rostum. *Turkische Kunst und Kultur aus osmanischer Zeit*. Frankfurt, 1985, 221-239.

The evolving culture of Kuwait. Edinburgh: HMSO, 1985.

Women's costume of the Near and Middle East. London: Unwin Hyman, 1987.

Ottoman Turkish Costume. *Costume* 22, 1988, 13-21.

The Art of Persian Lacquerwork. *British Antique Dealers Association Handbook*. 1989, 27-31.

The continuity of design techniques and motifs in Kutahya ceramics from the late 17th to the mid-20th century. *Proceedings of the First International Congress on Turkish Tiles and Ceramics*. Turk Petrol Vakfi Istanbul,1989, 231-246.

The Persian shawl industry. *The Textile Museum Journal* 27-28, 1989, 22-39.

The tradition of knotted pile carpets in Romania. *Oriental Carpet and Textile Studies* 3 (2), 1990, 211-225.

The Development of Women's Fashion in Ottoman Turkish Costume during the 18th and 19th centuries.In Taheusx Majda (ed), *Seventh International Congress of Turkish Art*. Warsaw: Polish Scientific Publishers, 1990, 199-206.

The Arts of the Eighteenth to Twentieth Centuries: Architecture, ceramics, metalwork, textiles. *The Cambridge History of Iran* 7, Cambridge University Press, 1991, 890-945.

Scott, J G. A Maori Carved Wooden Figure. *Scottish Art Review* VIII (1),1961, 13-15.

A Numori Figure from Sierra Leone,West Africa. *Scottish Art Review* VIII (1), 1961, 12.

Takemura, A. *Fukusa, Japanese Gift Covers*. Kyoto, 1991.

Trowell, M. *Classical African Sculpture*. London, 1954.

Wallis, W C. A Japanese Bronze Buddha in the Royal Scottish Museum. *Scottish Art Review* V (3), 1955, 31.

Wardwell, A. *The Art of Oceania*. The Art Institute of Chicago.

Wilkinson, J. Gordon Munro, "A Plea for Toleration". *Proceedings of the British Association of Japanese Studies*. Sheffield University, 1985.

Willett, F. The Hunterian Museum, its Founder and its Ethnographical Collection. *Quaderni Poro* 3, 1982, 85-94, reprinted in *Museum Ethnographers Group Newsletter* 14, 1983, 10-15.

Nigerian thorn-carvings: a living monument to Justus Akeredolu. *African Arts* 20 (1), 1986, 48-53, 98.